Eric Liddell's victory in the 400-meter race at the 1924 Paris Olympics was portrayed in the award-winning film, Chariots of Fire. Eric literally observed the Sabbath Commandment by refusing to run on Sunday. It cost him additional medals, and won him misunderstanding and criticism from the press.

God's Joyful Runner

reveals the untold story going beyond his Olympic competition, depicting the full depth of Eric's faith in God, commitment to service and compassion for others. His aim was not athletic achievement, but what he called his "incorruptible crown."

For twelve years, Eric taught at the Tientsin Anglo Chinese College under the sponsorship of the China Missionary Service. Later, he spent seven years as an itinerant rural missionary in China's Shantung Peninsula. Finally, during the latter years of World War II, Eric was interned with 1,800 other Christians at a compound in Weihsien. It was there, while continuing to offer encouragement to others, that Eric became seriously ill and died.

"Russ Ramsey has done the painstaking research that connects Father's life and writings to the greatness of the Christian missionary tradition . . . [God's Joyful Runner] is my father's story, his biography as authorized by Aunt Jenny (his sister) and his three daughters."
PATRICIA LIDDELL PATTERSON

God's Joyful Runner

Russell W. Ramsey, Ph.D.

*with joyful wishes
in Christ —*

Russell W Ramsey

BRIDGE PUBLISHING, INC. • SOUTH PLAINFIELD, NEW JERSEY

Scripture verses are taken from the King James Version.

GOD'S JOYFUL RUNNER

Copyright © 1987 by Bridge Publishing, Inc.
Library of Congress Catalog Card Number: 87-71167
Bridge Publishing, Inc., 2500 Hamilton Boulevard
South Plainfield, New Jersey 07080, USA

ISBN 0-88270-624-1

Printed in the United States of America
First printing: June 1987

Foreword

My father, Eric Liddell, shunned the limelight because he felt that he had not really done anything remarkable in his life.

My mother told me how, on one occasion following a big athletics meet, dozens of reporters were waiting for him. It was near the train station, so Father just borrowed a cap from an obliging porter, took over the fellow's cart, and pushed the luggage right through the crowd. No one knew who he was.

I think Father would be embarrassed about all this fuss, this publicity that comes from being the subject of three books, two motion pictures, many magazine articles; even the author of his own book. But if the complete telling of Father's story in this book helps just one soul along his spiritual journey, then it all will have been worthwhile.

There is a great scene in the movie *Chariots of Fire* where Ian Charleson, playing my father, comes tearing past the crowd in the Stade Colombe. The camera then moves up into the stadium and pans the crowd, zooming in on several girls all dressed up for the Paris heat at the 1924 Olympic Games, in the cloche hats and flapper outfits of the day.

It's a good scene because, throughout his life, my father encouraged girls to be all that they could become. Mrs. Elsa McKechnie Watson, at the age of fourteen, formed the Eric Liddell Club in Edinburgh, during the 1920s. She and her girls were prominently in evidence at many of my father's public speaking engagements.

Father taught the Sunday School class for the teenagers in Tientsin, China during the years as science teacher with the Tientsin Anglo-Chinese College. One of his starry-eyed pupils turned out to be my mother. During the hectic times that Father ministered to the rural Chinese when the Japanese occupation force was abusing them, I remember him coming in, dead tired, but always ready to play and joke with me and my baby sister, Heather.

Our father cycled all about the rural beat in the late 1930s, tending to his parishioners. People wondered at how he got about so well and so fast. I remember well the little seat that he rigged on his cycle, taking us about the streets of Tientsin with joy in his heart, even though we now know that things must have been a bit unsafe for foreigners.

In the Weihsien Prison Compound, my father became the science tutor for the secondary school pupils. One girl matriculated directly into a top Australian university in 1946, having been taught during three years' internment from notebooks that Father created by hand, from memory, since there were few books and no equipment.

What was it like to leave him? I remember well, on the dock at Tientsin, his reassuring smile, his loving words and embrace.

There was an old saying among the families of the London Missionary Society: "Those who love God never meet for the last time." How often I have thought of it since that day in 1940, and since that day in May 1945, when two men came to tell Mother that Father would not ever come home in this world.

Russ Ramsey has done the painstaking research that connects Father's life and writings to the greatness of the Christian missionary tradition. That place is now assured. This is my father's story, his biography authorized by Aunt Jenny (his sister) and his three daughters.

As his oldest daughter, I want everyone to know that my father, Eric Liddell, was the warmest, most loving and kindly father who ever lived. Those early childhood years with him were so tragically short. Yet Father's joyful faith has sustained my love for him all these years, and for all the years to come.

Patricia Liddell Patterson
Binbrook, Ontario, Canada
May 1986

Introduction

It may seem hard to grasp why there has been so much interest in Eric Liddell lately. There have been many medal-winning athletes and many inspiring missionaries. What makes Eric the type of person who has captured the hearts of millions through such media as the movie *Chariots of Fire,* the BBC documentary "The Flying Scot," and the Billy Graham Crusade's proposed film about Eric's ministry in northeast China?

He would probably deny that he was important enough to be remembered in films and biographies. He wasn't martyred for the faith, but he certainly poured out his life for the people he served. He won but a single Olympic gold medal, although it is very likely he would have won more at the 1928 Games if he had asked permission from the London Missionary Society to go. He wasn't a colorful, demonstrative, emotion-stirring preacher—he simply spoke about Jesus in a quiet, confident manner. Why then has this humble, committed man emerged as such a popular figure?

Perhaps the attention is due to revival of interest in the Olympic Games and Eric's giving up a chance at a medal in his premier event, the 100-meter sprint, because running on Sunday violated his personal religious practice. But he would not have considered this special. Many other Olympians, both British and American, forsook medal opportunities by refusing to compete in Sunday races.

Perhaps he is so intriguing because he was a Scot. There is a great deal of cross-cultural interest today in the United States and Britain. But Eric lived in Scotland for only five years of his life (plus two missionary furloughs of a few months each), and he spoke with a soft British accent, using only an occasional Scottish "wee bit" or "laddie."

Another appealing aspect of his life is his committed missionary service in China, especially under the savage conditions of banditry and war in the 1930s and '40s. Such courageous service is often well appreciated by the thousands of families who have lost loved ones in war. It seems clear, however, that Eric never intended to die under heroic conditions in Asia. All of his upbringing and schooling point strongly to his intention to spend his career in a quiet, sincere life of missionary teaching and conversion, as his father had done.

Possibly interest has been sparked by Eric's charisma and once immense popularity. In 1925, Eric's presence at an amateur track meet anywhere in Scotland was enough to insure a big crowd. His departure for the missions led to a spontaneous hymn-singing rally at Edinburgh's Waverley train station. The attendance at just one of Eric's rallies that year inspired a young man named Peter Marshall to commit himself to the ministry. Marshall eventually became Chaplain of the United States Senate, and his widow, Catherine, was one of America's well-known religious writers. Catherine freely attributed her husband's religious commitment to Eric's influence, and noted that Peter's ministry in America was his second choice—his first was to follow Eric into the China missionary service.

In reality, it is likely that all these factors contribute to contemporary interest in Eric. But since there are so many popular misconceptions about his life, and given our propensity for replacing heroes so quickly, the question that should be addressed at this point is whether Eric Liddell is a figure worthy of more than just the brief notoriety he has recently received.

The answer is undoubtedly yes. Eric Liddell is a truly compelling and inspiring figure whose historical importance transcends his own time.

In order to validate the assertion that Eric was a Christian for all ages, we need to study his entire life, not simply one or two isolated events, and take into account his own ideals and view of himself. We need to come to terms with these honestly, without bias or prejudice, and then let his true character emerge.

From his early youth, Eric primarily thought of his life as consecrated to bringing the gospel of Jesus Christ to the people of China. His remarkable athletic, teaching, and leadership gifts, charm and humor, dedication to family, and heroism in war need to be understood in light of this calling to which Eric responded. This is the context in which he viewed his own life and which brings into sharp relief the subsequent events he experienced.

This historically significant fact has often been misunderstood. One reason is that popular portrayals of Eric's life have cast events at slight variance with the facts for dramatic effect. More importantly, however, the tendency to minimize or recast religious elements in the lives of public figures has resulted in an imbalance. Today, strong religious convictions seem to be presented on the popular level only if they don't challenge or upset modern values, or if they appear only as quaint relics of the past.

Faith was the prime motivator in Eric Liddell's life. If we try to minimize or ignore the influence of his beliefs or his drive to spread the gospel, we will fail to understand him. We will likely also reduce him to the level of just another fleetingly interesting figure.

This fact may also turn away, or even frighten, some people from the story of Eric's life. Many of us think of such men as admirable but innately dull. But, though strongly religious, Eric was far from a stiff-shirted dogmatist. He was a man of many talents and interests, who fascinated his contemporaries and was well loved by them.

There is great value in examining such a man's life for both believer and skeptic. Eric Liddell's strong character will inspire us all and summon us to a better life. His example of dedication to high ideals makes him an outstanding model, and his witness of faith and love are a much-needed reminder to the modern world of true moral values.

There are also facets of Eric's life that have significance beyond our individual lives. We can use him as a foil to measure many current issues. He was in many ways the embodiment of the ideal athlete envisioned by Pierre di Fredi, the Baron Coubertin, the reviver of the modern Olympic Games. The French Baron resurrected the ancient Greek Games to bring together dedicated amateur athletes, whose athletic prowess served as a prelude to worthy, committed lives. Eric would surely disapprove of the commercialism and nationalism that threaten to undo the Olympic movement today. And he would even more strenuously oppose the absolute dedication to personal gain of many modern athletes. Athletics and the Olympics were never an end in themselves for Eric; they were a vehicle to bring God's message to others.

Dr. H.H. Almond, legendary Headmaster of the Loretto School near Edinburgh, part of the Rugby school movement, posed this question to his students in the late 1800s: "Why cannot there be a holy alliance between the athlete and the Christian; an alliance against the common enemies of both, against intemperance and indolence, and dissipation, and effeminacy, and aesthetic voluptuousness, and heartless cynicism, and all the unnatural and demoralizing elements in our life?" Eric's life demonstrated just such an alliance.

His life stands out also as truly representative of the power of the moral force that formerly linked East and West through Christian missionary efforts. For many, Eric is the symbol and substance of that link, and he is of the Olympic ideal. He brought the God of Calvary to both the people who worshiped the pagan gods of ancient Chinese cultures, and to those who worshiped human prowess at the foot of Mount Olympus.

I would like to thank Eric's sister, Jenny, and his eldest daughter, Patricia, for enabling me to bring Eric's complete story to the world. Patricia's "Foreword" explains that this book is sanctioned and approved as the one-time authorized biography of her father. Mrs. Elsa McKechnie Watson of Edinburgh gave valuable testimony of Eric's influence on Scottish youth. Professor Emeritus Neil Campbell told what Eric was like as a running partner, and General Sir Philip Christison, who was officer in charge of the pipeband of the Cameron Highlanders at the Paris Olympics, related Eric's views on the Games. The incomparable "Miss Annie" Buchan of Peterhead, Scotland, recalled at the age of ninety-three the final moments of Eric's life. John Hoyte of San Francisco related details of Eric's prison life even as he organized and led the 40th reunion visit of the Weihsien internment camp survivors in 1985.

John Keddie of the Church of Scotland was a tremendous source of detail on the ways that Eric applied scriptural truths to the art of sports competition. John has devoted his own life to the study and practice of Eric Liddell's serene version of "muscular Christianity." He acknowledges our debt to the Reverend D.P. Thomson, who assembled a documentary biography of Eric in 1971. Thomson, organizer of the great "muscular Christianity" rallies that swept Scotland in the early

1920s, was still around in 1954 when the young Reverend Billy Graham came in for the televised Holy Week Crusade.

It is no quaint accident of history that D.P. Thomson did the organizational work for Eric Liddell in 1923, and for Billy Graham in 1954. It is no accident that John Hoyte's grandfather and Eric Liddell's father trained for the China missionary service with the Dwight Moody "muscular Christians" of the 1890s. And it is surely no mere coincidence that my youngest son, Bobby Ramsey, wrote a letter to Jenny Liddell Somerville the day after he saw the film *Chariots of Fire*. Jenny's answer, now framed on Bobby's wall, told of Eric's beliefs in athletics as a way to show God's power in life. And I knew from that letter that I had to tell Eric's story. Jenny has kept up Eric's joyful witness for Christ with thousands of youths for half a century.

Jenny, Patricia, Miss Annie—and all the men and women touched by Eric's life—are calling us to the starting blocks. It is time to run the straight race, for this is the life of Eric Henry Liddell.

Part I

The Champion

His eyes stared ahead through the sultry afternoon haze while he dug two starting holes in the cinder track. Standing beside Eric Liddell for the Olympic 400-meter finals were the five fastest quarter-milers in the world—a fellow Brit, two Americans, a Canadian, and a Swede. Three of them had set new Olympic records during the previous twenty-four hours in the trial heats for the event. Liddell, in lane six, was not considered to be a contender for a medal, even though he was an accomplished 400-meter runner and had won two of his qualifying heats.

Eric was assigned a poor position at the starting line which was staggered to compensate for the turn in the track. From the outside lane it is very difficult to pace oneself against the other runners. Liddell was primarily a sprinter; his only chance would be to break out at top speed and hope to have the endurance to last the long distance. At his position Eric opened a note one of his trainers had handed him earlier in the day: "In the old book it says, 'He that honours me I will honour.' Wishing you the best of luck always."

"The Flying Scot," as he was known, then walked across the line shaking the hands of his competitors. As the Paris Stade Colombes buzzed with nervous excitement, someone joked that Liddell was saying good-bye; but few gave him a realistic chance.

At the gun, Eric sprinted out. Though he had run his fastest 400 meters just two hours earlier in the hot July sun, he led at the 200 mark in a blistering 22.2 seconds. No one expected he could maintain such a pace, and at the lone turn in the course Horatio Fitch of the United States appeared to move up on him. But in his characteristic style, Eric

3

threw his head back and reached down for all his physical and spiritual resources Two other runners fell and gamely got up again. Eric opened his lead in the final meters, and broke the tape in 47.6 seconds—a new Olympic and world record.

A sprinter winning a middle-distance event in the Olympics was a remarkable accomplishment. Eric became known worldwide and received a hero's welcome on his return to Scotland. At twenty-two years of age, his brilliant athletic career seemed to have just begun.

But Eric Liddell was more than just an athlete. Less than a year later he left the track to pursue his lifelong dream: missionary work in China. Years later in 1932 he was asked by a Toronto journalist if he regretted such an astounding decision: "Are you glad you gave your life to missionary work? Don't you miss the limelight, the rush, the frenzy, the cheers, the rich red wine of victory?"

"Oh, well," Eric replied, "of course it's natural for a chap to think over all that sometimes, but I'm glad I'm at the work I'm engaged in now. A fellow's life counts for far more at this than the other. Not a corruptible crown, but an incorruptible, you know."

Eric had always sought first the imperishable crown of salvation, not that of earthly glory, an image he borrowed from Paul's letter to the people of Corinth in A.D. 50. Eric Liddell ran every race to win, his eyes to the finish line. Scottish fans said he "culdna' lose when his heid's back." His quiet faith and humble, winning personality inspired countless numbers of people in his own day. But he knew that the crowns of athletic fame and popular admiration soon fade. Eric wasn't a man to spend his energy seeking worldly recognition; he was God's joyful runner, running out of love and deep desire for giving lasting glory to God.

If we try to understand his life without its spiritual foundation—isolating Eric as athlete, preacher, or hero/model—we may fail to grasp the essential element that brought all the facets of his life together and the guiding focus that he himself pointed to as the motivation behind all that he accomplished. From his youth, Eric primarily thought of his life as consecrated to the service and love of Jesus Christ, and particularly to bringing His message to the people of northeast China. It was his response to this call that led him to the Stade Colombes for the 1924 Olympic Games, as well as to the Shantung peninsula in China to preach the gospel.

Eric's deep love for God and for China came primarily from his parents. Both his mother and father were raised in Scotland but spent most of their lives as missionaries to China. The Reverend James D. Liddell and Mary Reddin were engaged in 1893. Each was twenty-two at the time, and they soon found they shared a strong faith and a desire to enter the foreign missionary service. When James applied to the London Missionary Society for duty in the Far East, they delayed the wedding until he was established in his mission. Even with the volatile political situation in the Orient and the discomfort and danger of missionary service, the application process was lengthy and highly selective. One reason for this was that the Society was completely funded by donation, and it was quite costly to send a missionary family halfway around the world. The prospective missionaries also had to prove that they were able to adapt to a new culture, learn a new language, survive amidst danger, and still be effective in preaching the gospel.

James continued his pastoral duties in his hometown of Drymen, located on the southeast corner of Loch Lomond, while he awaited the Society's reply. Mary, who was from Paxton, in Berwickshire, worked as a hospital nurse in Glasgow.

In 1898 the Society gave James Liddell a probationary assignment in Mongolia. New selectees were first sent into the field without their families to determine if they would be able to withstand the rigors of mission life. If they adapted well enough their families were then sent to join them.

After James left, Mary moved to the Isle of Lewis in the Hebrides to prepare herself for the role of missionary wife. She was far enough from home and in an appropriate environment to prepare for the demanding duties she would eventually face in China; but she was close enough to keep in touch with James by telegraph. Mary also began a practice that served to unite her family the rest of their lives, even in times of danger and separation: she habitually wrote lengthy letters that described local events and family news from the various places to which they were scattered.

James learned Chinese amazingly fast, and in just a few months secured permission to remain in China and to bring out his fiancée. They were married at the Shanghai Cathedral on October 23, 1899, and soon set about building a life in their new country.

The situation in the Far East was rapidly deteriorating at the turn of the century. In China, The League of Righteous and Harmonious Fists, known in Britian and America as "The Boxers" because of the karate-type drills they performed, was waging a revolt against the Manchu government and stirring up vehement anti-Western opposition. The Boxer Rebellion was caused in part by social unrest among the thousands of workers who had been displaced by industrialization and war. Boatmen lost their jobs on the Grand Canal when sampan transportation was replaced by ocean liners. Soldiers returned from defeat in the war with Japan and were unable to find work. Girls aged twelve to eighteen were being recruited by the thousands by Huang-lian Sheng-my, the Sacred Mother of the Yellow Lotus, for paramilitary revolutionary organizations such as the Red Lanterns.

The Boxers' doctrine was a negative reaction to Western technology and Christian ideas. One of their manifestoes proclaimed:

> To be converted to Christianity is to disobey Heaven, to refuse to worship our gods and Buddhas, and to forget our ancestors. If people act in this way, the morality of men and the chastity of women will disappear. To be convinced of this, one has only to look at their eyes, which are completely blue. . . . Our military strategy is simple: boxing [karate] must be learned so that we can expel the devils effortlessly; the railways must be destroyed, the electric wires severed, the ships demolished. All this will frighten France and demoralize Britain and Russia. The devils must be suppressed so that the Ch'ing [the dynasty that preceded the Manchus] empire may unite and celebrate peace. Kill the blue-eyed devils.

The Liddells' wedding occurred in the midst of this powerful social uprising. They left for the mission in Mongolia right after the ceremony, traveling by steamer to the Gulf of Po Hai and then by train and mule cart to the mission. By the following spring the Boxers and their sympathizers had forced the rural missionaries out. In their hasty flight the Liddells lost a trunk that contained priceless journal entries about life at the mission.

As such events mounted, the London Missionary Society seriously considered withdrawing all its staff from the country. The missionaries never shrank from danger, and often accepted martyrdom, but they did not deliberately remain in hopeless situations.

The situation grew worse for Westerners as the Manchu government desperately tried to retain control of the country. In addition to internal revolt, they had not regained the nation's confidence after the stinging defeat of the Sino-Japanese War of 1894-95. The Japanese, who had the advantage of internal control of the country and territorial integrity, had succeeded in converting to an industrialized economy before China. They were therefore able to strike a decisive blow in 1894 and to capture several coastal cities and destroy the incipient Chinese navy. The Chinese sued for peace, and were forced by the Treaty of Shimonoseki in 1895 to give up Formosa and the Pescadores Islands, to recognize the independence of Korea, and to pay a war indemnity.

The government, in an attempt to win back public support, tried to transfer the blame to the Western diplomats and missionaries. They were convenient scapegoats. Some influential Chinese were already denouncing all western influence in their country, especially U.S. Secretary of State John Hay's Open Door Policy, which many saw as a scheme to profit from the best treaty ports without having to pay for local upkeep and defense.

James and Mary Liddell and their fellow missionaries experienced tremendous challenges working in such a volatile situation. The laborers in the mission villages were undergoing tremendous changes in their lives—their jobs were threatened by an onslaught of railroads, steam tugs, mechanical digging machines, telegraph systems, and other technological innovations, and their values were being increasingly attacked and rejected. Such fast-paced change and the intense drive of the government to modernize the people took its toll on their lives.

The Boxers launched an all-out attack on the government in June 1900. Peking (Beijing) and Tientsin (Tianjin)* were the hardest hit. The legation guards held out at Peking, but the Boxers held Tientsin against a western relief force of over two thousand men. The rebels also

---

* The system for translating Chinese names into English during Eric Liddell's lifetime was devised and codified by British scholars Thomas Wade and Herbert Giles. In 1958, Chinese scholars developed the more accurate Pinyin system of linguistic transliteration, which is the one most often used today. I have primarily used the Wade-Giles system in this book, and occasionally put the Pinyin form in parenthesis for clarity.

attacked the coastal town of Taku, at the head of the Gulf of Po Hai, but the allied forces of Britain, France, and the United States retained the Taku forts.

Over two hundred Westerners were executed by the Boxers during the Rebellion. Many missionaries were martyred, some of whom were tormented and abused by howling mobs before being killed. The murder of a German missionary prompted the German government to send a large relief force. It was too late to bring much help, although parts of this force were used to carry out reprisals in several towns. Overall, however, the allied troops conducted themselves in a disciplined, self-restrained manner as they recaptured Tientsin (July 14) and Peking (August 14).

That summer, on August 27, 1900, Mary Liddell gave birth to her first child, Robert Victor, in the London Missionary Society's compound in Shanghai. His first name was given after his paternal grandfather, and the middle name for the recently announced victory over the Boxers.

James Liddell was sent to the north that summer to try to reestablish the London Missionary Society station in remote Mongolia. He accompanied Colonel Wei, the commander of a small force of the Chinese Imperial Army that was dispatched on a security mission. Though the Rebellion was over and the major powers were conferring at the peace table, reprisal murders in the villages were commonplace, and law and order had broken down on a massive scale. Bandit units emerged in the back lands, as had existed following the Sino-Japanese War. James found things too strenuous even to write up his usual letters and journal reports, and he returned to Tientsin late in the spring.

By September the political settlements between the allied Western nations and China had been made. China paid another huge indemnity, Germany received a new treaty port, and the Chinese government was required to protect the legations and the Western enclaves in each city where they had a treaty presence. Russia moved itself into the power vacuum by dispatching forces to southern Manchuria.

For James and Mary Liddell, the most important outcome of the Boxer Rebellion was its impact on the China missionary service. The Rebellion greatly stirred Western interest in the missions. In the decade that followed over one thousand new missionaries were recruited and sent to China from America, and hundreds from Britain.

James Hudson Taylor's group, the China Inland Mission, paid the highest price during the Rebellion. Fifty-eight adults and twenty-one children—nearly one-third of all missionary casualties—came from his organization. The result was that they experienced the highest number of successful new recruits in their history in the following year. The Student Volunteer Movement recruited successfully on dozens of campuses and raised desperately needed funds. The Yale-in-China Mission was dedicated to the memory of alumnus Horace Pitkin, one of the missionaries executed by the Boxers. The Dwight L. Moody Crusade appeared before cheering crowds in dozens of auditoriums.

The China Inland Mission took advantage of the upsurge in evangelical support from the homeland to improve its facilities in Tientsin. They built a hospital, installed a preparatory college after the British model of education, and established a boarding school for the daughters of missionary families at the nearby seacoast town of Chefoo.

The preparatory college at Tientsin opened in the spring of 1902. It was founded by Dr. Lavington Hart, a man who was tremendously influential in Eric's missionary life. His credentials give some idea of the kind of intellectuals who were volunteering for the China missionary service in that era. Dr. Hart joined the London Missionary Society in China in 1895, at the age of thirty-four. He had already received a Bachelor of Science degree from the Sorbonne in Paris, an honors degree in natural science from Cambridge, and a doctorate in science from London University. He had also been a professor at Cambridge, and was well known there as a supporter of missionary work.

On January 16, 1902, Mary Liddell gave birth at the Tientsin Mission Hospital to her second son. En route to the christening, James and Mary discussed the selection of the child's name. They decided to honor the maternal grandfather and name their new son Henry Eric. When James was on his way to register Eric's birth, a colleague asked, "How, will the son of a missionary family look when he writes his initials H.E.L.?"

They made a discreet reversal and settled finally on the name of Eric Henry Liddell. He was a bright, cheerful baby, who brought joy to the missionaries after such a time of suffering.

*T*he *Reverend Liddell* had worked on the new family home at the Siaochang mission station during the weeks following Eric's birth. Theirs was one of four row houses, each made of brick, with a long veranda on both floors, front and back. Mary and James Liddell and their two little boys moved in during June 1902. Their house was faced in the front with field stone and the veranda flanked on both sides by a wide flight of stairs. Rob and Eric usually played on the veranda and in the front yard, with Mrs. Liddell or a Chinese nurse *(amah)* attending them nearby.

Behind the four houses of the London Missionary Society staff were the mission school, hospital, and the chapel. Eric's father presided over one of the two mission stations that served the densely populated plain south of Peking. The sister mission was miles away at Tsangchow, and it was an arduous journey of 140 miles or so from each station to the city of Tientsin. Peking is the northern apex of the large plain and is guarded by the port city of Tientsin. The Shantung peninsula is a rolling wheat and millet growing region about the size of Wales which spreads out to the south of these cities. Eric Liddell spent most of his life in this region.

There were about ten million people on the plain in his time, spread out through ten thousand villages mostly of a few hundred people each, and thousands of family farms and hamlets. Their crops were not unlike Scotland's grains, but the agricultural methods were totally different. The climate was much drier, and the temperature extremes greater. It was common for temperatrues to drop to zero degrees Fahrenheit and summer extremes to reach one-hundred-ten degrees Fahrenheit.

The Hopei Province, which encompassed this region, covered a large territory. From Tientsin it was a jolting six-hour train ride to Techou (Tehsien; also called Tehchow in Eric's day). The railroad paralleled the Yun Ho River, one of five rivers that meet at Tientsin and empty southeastward into the Gulf of Po Hai, also called Chihli. When Mary Liddell took her little boys to Siaochang in the summer of 1902, she had to finish the journey from Techou in a mule-drawn cart. They traveled forty miles west across the great plain toward the Tzuya (Tzewy) River, camping overnight. If the trip went well, they would reach Siaochang on the afternoon of the second day.

Eric was cared for by his Chinese *amah* while his mother cared for the sick at the mission hospital. His *amah* called him "Yellee," since "Eric" was difficult to pronounce.* The *amahs* were adult women with bound feet. They appear to be standing on white powder boxes in photographs because the bones of their feet had formed permanently with the front half bent underneath, and they had to walk on built-up pads on the upper surface of their feet.

Bound feet and the pigtails that men wore in those days were becoming less common at the beginning of the twentieth century. The forces of traditionalism never regained control in China after the Boxer Rebellion, when those who wanted to modernize the country could get the upper hand politically. The dowager empress Tzu-hsi of the Manchus returned to her throne in January, 1902, the month that Eric was born. But those who wanted to modernize China had acquired that same year a new leader who began organizing political forces both at home and abroad that eventually swept away the Manchus forever.

It is doubtful whether the missionaries at Siaochang could foresee such changes as they worked to build up the Christian base of converts in the northern plain.

Following a brief trip to Tientsin, Mary Liddell gave birth to a daughter on October 3, 1903. The daughter was christened Janet Lilian, but everyone called her Jenny. The family settled in for the winter in their home in Siaochang, where Rob and Eric spent the long hours playing together in their room on the second floor. When the boys

---

* Chinese words seldom begin with a vowel sound; and they don't often end with a consonant. The letter "r" intonates like an "l."

played outside, they wore Chinese padded quilt coats and wide-brimmed, round hats, which had a crown instead of the cone-shaped top usually seen in China.

In the summer of 1904 Mary Liddell took the three children to the coast of the Po Hai, where the London Missionary Society had a retreat home on a lovely stretch of beach at Pei-tei-ho. Rob and Eric splashed around in the warm, salt water shallows, dressed in one-piece bathing suits held up by shoulder straps.

When the Liddells visited the coast they were able to get news of world events from the daily newspapers at Tientsin, one of which was in English. There were also several large steamers that arrived or departed each week, and a reliable telegraph service that connected the city with Europe. The Reverend Liddell was able to join his family for a month's holiday in August. Since the members of the church needed everyone in their families for the intensive hand labor of the harvest season, so the attendance at Christian church activities in Siaochang therefore declined heavily.

They were astounded to hear that summer that Japan, which just fifty years before had been a small hermit kingdom, had gone to war with Russia. At the time, maritime territories to the north of Japan were the only ones in dispute, but the missionaries noted sadly that both parties coveted Manchuria, which they believed China could not defend against modern armed forces. They later shared the amazement of the rest of the world when Japan's navy destroyed Russia's Asian fleet in the Sea of Japan.

The winter of 1904-05 was a good one for the Siaochang mission. The Chinese government strongly supported education because they saw it as a necessary precondition to modernization.

The government's move to improve Chinese education appeared to take an upturn in 1905 with the appointment of a Minister of Education at Peking. But in just a few months thousands of China's brightest young minds were sent abroad to study, most of whom enrolled in Japanese universities. The overseas student community in Japan later became a hotbed of revolutionary sentiment against the imperial monarchy. The following year the Empress announced a comprehensive set of reforms which included adopting a constitution based on a study of those from several foreign countries. However, except in remote provinces that had strong warlords, Manchu princes were put in charge of the reforms, and so the process of change was considerably slowed.

News reached the Liddells on their summer holiday of 1906 about a new Scottish track star who had distinguished himself at an unexpected sporting event. A dispute had arisen following the First Olympiad between the city of Athens, which hosted the 1896 games, and Baron Pierre de Coubertin, who had revived the ancient Greek Olympics. The Athenians wanted to be the permanent hosts of the Olympic Games, but Coubertin had refused, believing it was necessary to rotate the Games among host countries to develop a true base of international support for the movement. The Greeks were aware that cyclical regional Games among the ancients were on both a two-year and four-year basis, and they saw no reason not to offer international Games of their own sponsorship. Coubertin, of course, was not in favor, but the only thing he could do was to deny the official sanction of the International Olympic Organizing Committee.

The government of Athens decided to mark the tenth anniversary of the Paris Conference that founded the modern Olympic Games by hosting their own Games in 1906. These became known afterwards as the Intercalated Games of 1906. Though they were not sanctioned by the International Olympic Organizing Committee, they were better attended and better run than either the 1900 Paris or 1904 St. Louis Games. The Liddells most likely didn't know much of the controversy surrounding the Games, but the young Scot they had heard of was Army Lieutenant Wyndham Halswelle, who had won the silver medal in the 400-meter race. Though the 1906 Games are not considered official, Halswelle became the first Scot to win a medal in Olympic track and field competition.

James and Mary Liddell knew that after that winter the idyllic family life with their three young children at Siaochang had to change. Sons of the London Missionary Society were educated in England at Eltham, and Rob was already at the age when boys matriculated. Furthermore, missionaries normally took furloughs home after seven years in the field. The Reverend Liddell was overdue for his first return to Drymen, where he was expected to make deputation appearances to gain material and prayerful support for the missions. They all yearned to see the family at home, but were saddened by the thought that Eric and Rob would not come back with them.

In the spring of 1907, Rob and Eric said good-bye to China. They were neither Scots nor Chinese, they were London Missionary Society boys. They both loved China and hoped to return one day as they boarded the coastal steamer at Tientsin to begin their long voyage "home."

*J*ames and Mary Liddell had their hands full on the long voyage to Southhampton with three children aged six, five, and three. Little Rob, Eric, and Jenny had never seen the land of their parents' birth, nor had anyone in Scotland ever seen the three children, who spoke about as much Chinese as English.

Eric was still recovering from a terrible case of dysentery during the voyage. Mary had nursed him for weeks on a special diet of Valentine's concentrated beef juice, which came in cans all the way from England. Dysentery often was fatal in those days, and the recovery was slow. Eric languished for weeks pale, drawn, weak, and stumbling about to such an extent that one of the missionary wives remarked, "That boy will never be able to run."

After the ship docked, the Liddell family took the overnight train to Edinburgh and then traveled west to Glasgow where there was a joyous welcome from the family at Drymen. The young family spent the summer in James Liddell's hometown. Eric's paternal grandfather ran a grocery store in the village and operated a wagonette drawn by a small white pony. His normal fare to carry passengers from the train station to the village was sixpence.

The Liddell family in Drymen belonged to an evangelistic tradition. Their favorite hymns were collections from two Americans, Dwight L. Moody and Ira David Sankey. Sankey's unforgettable lyrics and tunes, which were always Eric's favorites, were published from 1875 to 1891 as *Gospel Hymns*. The family's religious background influenced James' decision to enter the theological college of the Scottish Congregational Church. The church had beliefs similar to those of the Calvinist

Presbyterians of the National Church of Scotland, but it stressed local control of church affairs by the individual congregation. It was one of the church's missionaries, the Reverend William Blair, who most influenced James Liddell's desire to take the gospel overseas. Blair was doing his deputation work at Helensburgh, a town in southwest Scotland where the Clyde River meets the sea, and where young J.D. Liddell was on vacation. He attended one of the Reverend Blair's public meetings and decided to quit his job installing draperies for the theological college.

Many people are familiar with early twentieth-century life in Scottish villages like Drymen through the novels by Dr. A.J. Cronin, who paints an artistic but unfair picture of Scotland in the early 1900s. Drymen's shopkeepers were not unpleasant creatures like James Brodie in *The Hatter's Castle,* and missionaries who went out to China were not pietistic klutzes like Father Francis Chisholm in *Keys of the Kingdom,* nor insincere organizational climbers like Father Chisholm's colleagues. Love, humor, sincerity, commitment, and integrity better describe the Reverend James Liddell and his family in Drymen.

Rob and Eric started school in the fall of 1907 at Drymen as day students, while living at home with their family. Jenny was too young for school at the time. James and Mary decided, however, that the boys needed to go on down to Eltham at Blackheath, the excellent boarding school near London where the sons of the China missionary service lived and studied while their parents were overseas. After only sixty years of operation, the school already numbered the sons of the missionary giants David Livingstone and James Gilmour among its alumni, and had established a firm foundation in the Christian scholar-athlete preparatory tradition. A measure of its success is that a large majority of the graduates, who knew firsthand about the difficulties of life as a missionary, chose to continue in the tradition of the gentle knights of the foreign missionary service.

Rob and Eric shared a room at Eltham College. They began their careers in team sports immediately, though Rob was not yet eight and Eric was only six. James returned alone to Siochang, and Mary and Jenny remained behind for a year to make sure the boys settled in all right. She and Jenny joined James in September 1909.

Mary Liddell remembered her last sight of her boys in the carriage that took her back to the train station. They were down below on a playing field, totally absorbed in a game of cricket, and did not even see the family drive away. That night, however, Eric cried himself to sleep, having spent very few nights of his life apart from his mother. It was five years until they were again united.

Life at Eltham consisted of studies, group activities, religious guidance, and sports. In the summer of 1908 interest in sports reached a high pitch, because the City of London was hosting the IVth Olympiad. On July 7, 1908, King Edward the VIIth opened the Games at White City Stadium. There were the finest Games to that date, and it is no exaggeration to say that the London Olympic Organizing Committee saved the Olympic movement from probable extinction.

An event at the 1908 Olympics impressed itself so strongly on Eric's young mind that he quoted it all his life. The Bishop of Pennsylvania preached in St. Paul's Cathedral at London, quoting for his text a motto over the gate at the University of Pennsylvania. "In the dust of defeat, as well as in the laurels of victory," ran the motto, "there is a glory to be found if one has done his best." Not all the Modern Olympiads exhibited that kind of idealism.

The city of Athens had done surprisingly well in staging the first modern Olympiad in 1896, though the participation of the British athletes was soured by the fact that Oxford and Cambridge decided not to participate. And the IId Olympiad at Paris had embarrassed Baron de Coubertin terribly in his own country. The organizing committee there saw the Games as a sideshow to the Universal Exposition of French Science and Commerce held at Paris during the same weeks. The IIId Olympiad was hardly better at St. Louis in 1904. It was attended by only ten countries, and only 92 of the 625 athletes who competed were from countries other than the United States. The Olympic Games also were mixed in with entertainment events and exhibits of the World's Fair which commemorated the centennial of the Louisiana Purchase. Baron de Coubertin did not even attend the Games and, not surprisingly, American runners dominated the events.

The game in which boys of the British boarding schools learned sportsmanship, teamwork, and courage was rugby. Named for the school where the British educational tradition was shaped by Dr. Thomas Arnold, the game had evolved by 1908 into an important social force. Two kinds of football were played in Britian—rugby, which was called "football" or "rugger," and soccer, which also was called "football" or "association football." Rugby teams had fifteen players on a side and used a combination of passing, kicking, and ball carrying. The game utilized a ball that resembled an American football with too much air in it, and featured more running and less damaging tackles than its American counterpart. Towns and schools had highly organized leagues in both rugby and soccer. While Rob and Eric played both, "rugger" was clearly their first love. W.B. Hayward, the Headmaster at Eltham, conducted two rugby seaons per year, with three or four games per week.

Rob and Eric's parents and sister went back to a China that was changing rapidly. Life at Siaochang was not changed substantially for several more years, but different political events soon affected them and the entire nation. In 1905 a medical doctor, Sun Yat-sen had formed the National People's Party, or Kuomintang. This party advocated autonomy in China's national life, democracy, and a guaranteed income for all citizens. They were strongest in the treaty ports, where Manchu control was weak, and they had many members among China's huge overseas student community. In mid-November the dowager empress, Tzu-hsi, and her emperor died, which left a Regent and an infant prince to rule for the Manchu dynasty.

Mary Liddell quickly established her custom of writing letters to her boys to keep them emotionally and spiritually close to their family. Rob took the lead in the boys' replies, but Eric also began communicating with the family by mail.

Sports and boarding school food toughened Eric up after his bout with dysentery. The boys mainly ate porridge, bread and butter, and milk for breakfast with jam or marmalade as an occasional treat. The other meals consisted of bread and butter, or bread with meat and gravy. Fruit was served on special occasions. Evidently Eric was none too fond of meat pudding, for he was occasionally punished for concealing unswallowed fat in his mouth and then spitting it out when he returned to his room.

After a few weeks of shyness, Eric established a reputation for manly behavior that marked him for special affection all his life. He did most of the pranks that the other boys did, and at times thought up a few of his own. He never lied when caught, but he wouldn't tattle-tale on another boy either. And he became the champion of the underdog.

Hazing did exist in the British boarding school system, though one of Dr. Thomas Arnold's reforms had been to clean up its more abusive forms. Eric decided to take a stand against it when he was eight years old. A new boy was being made to run down a double line of older boys, who snapped at him with their knotted handkerchiefs. The little boy looked pitifully at Eric, who quietly confronted bigger lads of ten or eleven. The hazing would stop, he said. And it did!

The boys from the London Missionary Society usually had very little money, so during the holidays, when the small staff of resident Masters had some free time, the boys stayed with volunteer families in or around London. Having the Eltham boys in their homes was part of Christian missionary service for these families, and it was an important dimension of Eric's life. On longer holidays, Rob and Eric took the train to stay with relatives at Berwick-on-Tweed, which is just below the Scottish border, or to Drymen to visit their father's two sisters.

Eric demonstrated a sense of humor and a personality of his own at school which showed clearly that, although Rob was an important guiding force in his life, he was a strongly independent boy. When his form level (class) did Lewis Carroll's *Alice in Wonderland,* Eric played the Doormouse. The audience broke up laughing at his earnest portrayal of the farcical role. Eric's nickname, "The Mouse," lasted for several months. Lewis Carroll, a graduate of Rugby and Oxford, wrote the story for a young girl by the name of Alice Liddell, but Eric was never able to determine if she was a relative.

Eric also was noticed because he exhibited courtesy and eagerness at the same time. He never took a smaller boy's turn away at the playground slide. Indeed, he often interfered on a smaller boy's behalf if someone else tried. But when Eric's turn came to slide, he leaped into action with a kind of grace and joy that warmed the hearts of the strict but loving British school staff.

A classmate wrote years later, when Eric's exhortations at student evangelical gatherings were well known, that Eric had shown even at the age of ten a remarkable integration of mind, body, and soul. He was everyone's friend; but, except for Rob, he never had a single chum with whom he was uniquely close.

By the time Eric was eight years old, Eltham was outgrowing its facility. At the same time, First Sea Lord Jackie Fisher was rapidly expanding the Royal Navy and so declared the Royal Naval School at Mottingham insufficient to house those in training. The school was perfect for Headmaster W.B. Hayward's needs, and in 1912 the move was consummated. Eltham College at Blackheath then became known as Eltham College at Mottingham, or just Eltham. There were several buildings in the complex including Fairy Hall, which had classrooms, Masters' quarters, and dorms; the King George Dining Hall; a library and a science laboratory; a dispensary and a chapel; and playing fields for rugby, cricket, and running. Day students were admitted and so the college also increased its staff.

On February 12, 1912, the Manchu dynasty was overthrown in China. The Kuomintang begun by Dr. Sun Yat-sen came to power, and the Presidency was assumed by Yuan Shih-k'ai three days later. There was no anti-missionary dimension to this revolutionary change, and Mrs. Liddell wrote Rob and Eric that everything was fine at Siaochang. By summer she was expecting again, and on December 4, 1912, Ernest Blair Liddell was born.

Events in the Far East over the next two years foreshadowed what was to come. Yuan Shih-k'ai consolidated his power and proclaimed himself president of China for ten years in 1914. Japan was continuing to build up its fleet and its plans for territorial expansion on the mainland. As James and Mary Liddell steamed towards Britain in 1914 with Jenny and little Ernest on their second furlough, the threat of war was settling on Europe.

The Headmaster at Eltham, W.B. Hayward, retired that same year from the school where Eric Liddell had already learned many of the values that characterized his entire life. He was learning at the little college that the quality of a person's struggle to achieve ultimately counts for more than winning the race.

"*Eric was entirely* without vanity, yet he was enormously popular. Very early he showed signs of real character. His standards had been set for him long before he came to school. There was no false pride about him, but he knew what he stood for." So wrote George Robertson, who became Headmaster at Eltham in 1914. He was quite fond of Eric and was one of the primary influences on his developing character.

Headmaster Robertson wasn't beyond the reach of Eric's sense of humor, however. He had made a rule against bicycling in the quadrangle at Ferry Hall, because of the narrow entrance archway and heavy pedestrian traffic. One afternoon, when there was hardly anyone around, the "Head" broke his own rule. He put his son in the front handlebar basket of his bicycle and took a ride through the campus.

"Hey," a voice called out an upper story window, "no cycling there!"

Robertson knew his boys, their voices, and which boy went with each window. Eric was sent to bed without supper that night.

The most determinative continuous influence on Eric, other than his brother Rob, was his science teacher Professor A.P. Cullen, who had joined the staff at Eltham in 1909 before the move to Mottingham. Cullen was the only person physically with Eric during the three major periods of his life: his youth, athletic career, and missionary service. The last was when they served together on the staff at the Tientsin Anglo-Chinese College.

Eltham College was the students' family in those years. The fact that the students had little money made them dependent upon the school to fill their time and their needs. Long letters from the family helped fill the void, but the onset of World War I restricted both their travel and the number of things they could do. Headmaster Robertson made sure nonetheless that his boys had a program that included social contact with the outside world. He knew his task was to educate future missionaries, so he wanted them to be able to work with many different types of people. They would spend their lives working with people, and would be expected to spend part of their lives teaching people in the homeland about the missionary service.

One of the most popular outings with the boys was the the Baths (swimming pools) at Ladywell. Most people in those days didn't swim when they went into the water. Rob and Eric, however, soon learned to swim laps in the manner of competitive swimmers. They were both fast and might have been excellent racing swimmers if competition swimming pools had been more available.

The boys also were known to clown around a bit at the Ladywell Baths. A favorite spoof was feigning the award of the British "Order of the Bath," which was a beautiful, ribboned medallion awarded by the Crown to worthy gentlemen for distinguished service, while draped in wet towels. Eric would repeat this spoof at Edinburgh, years later, when he was a national celebrity.

Another favorite activity was picking strawberries at the estate of Mr. A.P. Vinson, who had a son at Eltham. They also occasionally visited the homes of the day students who were added to Eltham under Robertson's Headmastership.

But the biggest event of 1914 for Rob and Eric was the arrival of their family, including their brother Ernest, whom they had never seen.

They had a family reunion at Drymen and many outings in the Scottish villages getting reacquainted after the long separation. The Reverend Liddell undertook vigorous deputation work while his wife went down to Mottingham in early 1915 to rent a furnished house. Rob and Eric retained their room at the college, but they were able to stay with their mother and brother and sister during the holidays for nearly a year.

Mrs. Liddell also had another goal in mind for being near London. Jenny, who would soon be twelve, needed schooling of a more advanced level than the family was able to provide at the little mission station in Siaochang. It must have been wrenching for any missionary wife to consider leaving her only daughter in the home country, but the Liddells planned to leave Jenny at Walthamstow, the school for girls the missionaries had been operating near London since before the turn of the century.

Walthamstow was close to Eltham. In fact, Eric was once supposed to play in a tennis match between the two schools, but was too shy to compete with the girls, and so refused. Women were not ordained as ministers in the missionary service in those days, and the missionaries were financially hard pressed to educate even their sons, the next generation of overseas evangelists. Nevertheless, the wives and daughters of the missionaries quite regularly worked overseas as teachers and nurses. The missionaries in China had established a boarding school for their daughters at Chefoo, a delightful town on the Gulf of Po Hai (Chihli), but the Liddells hoped that Jenny would take well to Walthamstow. If they had to keep three of their children halfway around the world, at least they would be close together.

The world situation was undoubtedly a factor in the minds of James and Mary Liddell. The British Expeditionary Force already was taking high casualties in the war against Germany. The Japanese government forced the "Twenty-one Demands" upon China in 1915, a humiliating treaty that gave Japan great trading advantages in China and a "sphere of influence" in Manchuria. Further, the efforts of the new Chinese Republic to participate in World War I were viewed by leaders on both sides mainly in terms of how they could get new forms of advantage in China. In addition, there were constant revolts, warlord struggles, and outbreaks of banditry that the new government was not able to control.

Jenny was able to spend time with her brothers and to enjoy some of their athletic prowess during her short time at Mottingham. Eric once confided to her after he had done poorly on a form examination and then excelled on the track, "I don't think much of the lessons, but I can run."

In February of 1915 it was time for Mary and Ernest to rejoin James Liddell, who had already gone to Siaochang. Jenny was settled in at Walthamstow, and said some tearful farewells to her mother and youngest brother. But as Mrs. Liddell was preparing to leave for the train in Southhampton, she received an urgent message to return to Walthamstow. The Headmistress told her that Jenny was simply too unhappy, and that she should return to China with her mother. She showed great depth of understanding by telling Mrs. Liddell how some girls at Walthamstow who were left there from their early years were emotionally closer to women faculty members than to their own mothers by the time of "passing out" (graduating).

So Jenny sailed for China with her mother and Ernest. Since her father was soon to be transferred to new duties in Peking (Beijing), Jenny was sent to the school for girls in Chefoo.

Mrs. Liddell loved the new assignment in Peking, where there was a complete European community and all the charming dimensions of missionary life in China. Peking and Chefoo were linked by regular steamer service, so she was able to see Jenny regularly during school holidays.

World War I had many effects on Eltham. Eighteen-year-old boys left for military service, with the great admiration of the younger boys, and so opportunities for athletics and social leadership among boys in their mid-teens were greatly expanded. Eric was a favorite with staff members who conducted the voluntary Bible study classes. He seldom missed them, even though attendance was not required, and his teachers noted that he paid close attention and knew the content of each lesson. While he did not say much, he often encouraged the teacher by constant eye contact and friendly nods and smiles.

Eltham managed to get in a full season of varsity athletics in 1916 despite the inroads the war was making on the student population and the availability of resources. Though cricket was not Eric's favorite game because of the many long periods of waiting and the lack of the social interaction he loved in rugby, he was nevertheless a good fielder and could run like the wind. Eric earned his "colours," the British cricket equivalent of a high school letter, at the age of fourteen. Rob, sixteen months older, had won his first "colours" the previous year and was generally considered to be a better cricketeer than Eric.

In the fall rugby season of 1916, Eric got his chance to play on the varsity team because several older boys had left for military service. Though light, he was very fast. The natural position for him was the three-quarter wing, which mainly requires the player to streak up and down the outside flanks watching for opportunities to drive inside for the score. Ball handling and fast playmaking are the essence of the three-quarter wing, which equates in some ways to the offensive end in American football. The position also requires defense against the fastest players on the opposing team. Eric had great speed, lightning coordination, and the determination needed to bore in for smother tackles.

That year Eric earned his "flannels," the equivalent of a varsity letter in rugby. The young prep school team did not have the kind of highly-skilled athletes who could feed the ball to a fast three-quarter wing, so Eric wasn't involved in much scoring. He also played on the tennis team in 1916 and was quite active in social life.

Though Eric still refused to participate in "ragging" the younger boys if it included physical abuse, he was not above more clever rituals in which the new boys were required to do all sorts of imitations to amuse the older ones. Someone blew the whistle on them, however, and Headmaster Robertson called the guilty to account. Throughout the inquisition Eric wore the same cherubic smile that he always had, until he was implicated in the affair.

"Liddell," the Headmaster said, "I am beginning to think you are not as good as you look."

One of the Masters demanded punctilious answers to his questions. Eric was always verbally shy and gave his answers quietly, but this master mistook his quietness for a lack of enthusiasm. The proper response, he told Eric, was to answer with a vigorous "sir" on the end. Eric did not talk back; he merely answered with an exaggerated "sir" the next time he was called upon. He deflated pompousness with gentle resistance of this kind.

Eric's courses were tougher in 1917, and Eltham cancelled its interscholastic athletics season because of the war. The cricket and rugby teams trained by playing intramural and scratch matches with local clubs, and Eric improved his athletic prowess. His rugby technique also improved tremendously. He became known as a fast smother tackler, his kicking gained accuracy, and he learned how to fall on the ball and hold it. However, while all six of the Eltham House Masters knew Eric well and saw him play sports regularly, not one of them predicted greatness for him either in rugby or in running.

In 1917 Eric was confirmed with a group of boys from Eltham in the Scottish Congregational Church, which had a direct supporting relationship with the college and the London Missionary Society. The newly-confirmed boys started their own Communion Service and participated in the meetings of the Crusaders' Union, a student evangelical organization. Eric became a volunteer worker with the Islington Medical Mission, starting a practice of ministering to the sick in institutions that he continued all his life. Rob was already hoping to attend Edinburgh University's renowned medical college and had pretty well made up his mind about what he wanted to do with his life.

Headmaster Robertson did manage to conduct a varsity athletics season for his teams in 1918. Eric was the vice-captain in cricket, and of the rugby team. No one doubted, now, that a rugby star was developing at the little college. Eric set a blistering personal example, running all over the field at high speed, making excellent smother tackles, and winning several games for Eltham with dazzling scoring drives. He seemed to have one weakness as captain in that he would not scold a team member who was putting out less than full effort. But Eric exercised his role of leadership through quiet words of encouragement and personal example, eschewing the part of the shouting, gesticulating field general.

In track, Rob and Eric were each stars. The Senior Championship, an intrasquad track meet with points awarded for first, second, and third place in each event, was held each year at the end of the season. A cup was awarded to the athlete with the highest overall score. Eric tied the school record in the 100-yard dash with a time of 10.8 seconds, beating Rob by a step. Eric also won the 440-yard race and the long jump, with Rob winning the steeplechase, the high jump, and the hurdles race. The Liddell brothers had captured first or second in all six of these premier track events, and Rob had won the overall Senior Championship.

Rob was ineligible for the Blackheath Cup in 1918, the prize annually awarded to Eltham's best overall athlete, because he had won it the previous year. So Eric, at the unprecedented age of sixteen, won the Cup in 1918.

Many things changed after the war ended in November of 1918, and the soldiers flooded back to Britain. Athletic competition became tougher, for one thing, and Rob and Eric witnessed the effects of soldiers' return on an economy that could not quickly adapt to the sudden influx. They saw in the greater London environment both the victorious parades and the uglier side of what happened after the Great War. There were frequent riots among the veterans, including men on the streets with heart-rending scars and missing limbs. Many men did

28

not return at all, including the Scottish track star Captain Wyndham Hallswelle, who had died in battle.

In the wake of World War I, the China missionary service experienced another spurt of growth and evangelical fervor. In 1919 Professor Cullen, who had brought science alive for Eric in the classroom, went to China and joined the staff at the Tientsin Anglo-Chinese College. Students in Peking were demonstrating at the time against their government's acceptance of the Peace Treaty, which they saw as continuing the same disadvantageous, humiliating relationships with the European Allies and Japan that existed before she entered on the Allied side.

Rob left Eltham for Medical College at Edinburgh University in 1918. It boasted such famous alumni as America's Dr. Benjamin Rush, Charles Darwin (naturalist), Joseph Lister and James Syme (antisepsis pioneers), and James Y. Simpson (chloroform's medical pioneer). Rob joined medical students from all over the British Empire, as well as a bumper crop of Scottish medical trainees from the war.

Eric came into his own as a campus leader after his brother left Eltham. He was a School Prefect, a role in which he exhibited a talent for fairness and tact, and captain of both the cricket and rugby teams. His friend and rugby model, A.L. Gracie, had returned from army service that year. Gracie was the college's top athlete when he left Eltham for military service in 1917. He was awarded the Military Cross in France, which is roughly equivalent to the U.S. Army Distinguished Service Cross. He and Eric set up a high speed quarterwing combination that made the Eltham rugby team competitive with much larger colleges. On the track, Eric set a school record in the 100-yard sprint with a time of 10.2 seconds. He also won the 1919 Senior Athletics Championship (track), which Rob had won the year before.

While Eric was extremely popular and respected, he was not considered Eltham's top student. The students voted annually to award the Bayard Prize to the boy who most influenced others during the year. During Eric's last two years, his brother Rob and war hero A.L. Gracie won this honor. The faculty selected a Head Boy in the top form each year, and in 1920 A.L. Gracie received this designation.

By the early weeks of 1920, Eric had cleared all his examinations for matriculation at Edinburgh University with the exception of French. In March he went up to share a temporary room with Rob, full of excitement about starting university life and about some news from China. His mother was due to arrive with Jenny and Ernest in April, and his father would come on furlough a few months afterward. A tutor was engaged to drill Eric in French, and he and Rob looked around for a furnished house in the University district for the family. Eric needed a bicycle and money for college so, in the summer of 1920, he took a job as a farmhand just on the outskirts of the city.

In April, Eric and Rob had a joyous reunion with Mother, Jenny, and Ernest at the huge Waverley train station. Rob and Eric took them by carriage to a house at 21 Gillespie Crescent, which still is in use in a quiet residential neighborhood.

Thus, in the summer of 1920, Eric got up very early to do the farm work; Rob was deeply engrossed in his medical studies, which a student, in those days, could enter directly without first passing through a separate undergraduate program; Ernest enrolled in a day school; and Mary Liddell had all four of her children living together with her for the first time in five years.

"*A* *new luminary* of the first magnitude has appeared in the firmament," opined a writer for the Edinburgh University undergraduate magazine after the annual University Sports, an intramural track meet on May 28, 1921 at the Craiglockhart sports complex in Edinburgh. Eric Liddell began to make his mark in athletics his first year in Edinburgh.

He enrolled at Heriot Watt College in the fall of 1920. Eric's house on Gillespie Crescent was less than a mile below the Edinburgh Castle; he pedaled his bicycle about one-and-one-half miles to classes, which were at the corner of Cowgate and George IV Bridge. Rob's classes at the Medical College were about two blocks to the south. Heriot Watt specialized in science and, like the Medical College, had a long list of distinguished world class scientists among its graduates. Each school was somewhat independent but allowed cross enrollment with Edinburgh University.

The Olympic Games, which had been cancelled in 1916 because of the Great War, were splendidly revived during the summer of 1920 in Antwerp. Eric and Rob were quite interested in the international sporting event. The British-American rivalry was stronger than ever, but the presence of military veterans at the Games, men who had so recently been allies on a real battlefield, diffused some of the tensions that had arisen in past Olympics.

American athletes had dominated the early Olympiads, but in the 1908 London Games runners from the British Empire surprised the American track and field juggernaut with victories in both the 100-meter and the 200-meter races. A dispute arose, however, when the Americans

31

used team tactics in the 400-meter run to block out Wyndham Halswelle, the favorite and a London-born Scot. Near the end of the race, J.C. Carpenter of Cornell University moved in front of Halswelle, blocking his kick at the finish. The Americans believed that this practice was legal, though they had been told beforehand that British track officials would not accept it.

A British official then broke the tape and declared the race void. Carpenter was disqualified and the London Olympic Organizing Committee ordered the race to be rerun the following day. W.C. Robbins and John Taylor of the United States both refused to compete, however, believing that their teammate had been wronged in an act of national partisanship. Halswelle ran the race alone the next day in journeyman time. Bitterness between the two teams was greater thereafter. British fans believed that Hallswelle had been wronged and then deliberately humiliated the following day by a blatant act of bad sportsmanship.

The Baron de Coubertin later wrote, "The circumstances . . . pitted the youth of the two Anglo-Saxon (nations) against one another with particular virulence, and gave birth within the Olympic body to a kind of test of muscular strength between their champions." British and American sports leaders, when the emotion subsided, searched for some deeper values than mere winning at all costs. The games were somehow not meeting the high ideals that the Bishop of Pennsylvania had quoted in the motto over the gate.

For the 1920 Antwerp Games, Coubertin introduced some fine pageantry that set a tone of Olympic idealism thereafter. The new Olympic flag was presented, consisting of a white field with five linked rings. The rings were red, green, black, yellow, and blue, representing at least one color from every flag in the world, and reminding the participants of the truce from all disputes and wars which the Trojans and the Eleans enforced while the Games were held at Olympia. The new Olympic Pledge also was made official. One athlete recited the pledge for all: "In the name of all competitors, I promise that we will take part in these Olympic Games, respecting and abiding by the rules which govern them, in the true spirit of sportsmanship, for the glory of sport and the honor of our teams." The athletes at ancient Olympia also took an oath, but it was even sterner and was made en masse by the athletes in the name of Zeus.

The Brits made sure there was no "boxing in" at Antwerp. Albert Hill, a remarkable thirty year old British Army veteran, won the 800- and 1,500-meter runs that year, the first man ever to double in those events. Philip Baker, the British team captain (Commandant), ran the 1,500 meters with Hill, letting it be known to all that he was running to keep anyone from blocking Hill. Baker succeeded, and even won the silver medal. Baker played a significant role in easing the tensions and restoring a spirit of sportsmanship between the two teams. It was no accident that he had studied at Haverford College in America as a young man, and was well aware of the motto atop the gate at the University of Pennsylvania. He later became involved in working for world peace, and was awarded the Nobel Peace Prize in 1959 for his world disarmament plan. He said at the ceremony, "It is many years since I first discovered that Englishmen were wrong in thinking that Americans were bad sportsmen, and also discovered that international contests led not to friction, but to friendship."

The American and British teams again dominated the Olympic track events in 1920. Charley Paddock from Texas won the 100-meter sprint and captured the silver medal in the 200 meters. Americans were first and second in each sprint, but Britain's Harry Edward was a close third in the 100 and again in the 200 meters. In the 400-meter race, Bevil Rudd from South Africa won the gold medal and Britain's Guy Butler was second. Edinburgh University students followed these events at the Antwerp Olympics closely.

Rob and Eric were both strong competitors, but also fine sportsmen. Family teachings and twelve years at Eltham College had instilled in them values like that in 2 Timothy 2:5: "And if a man also strive for masteries, yet is he not crowned, except he strive lawfully."

The two young men during the fall of 1920 became regular participants in the services and classes at the Morningside Congregational Church, which was just down the street from their house. Rob had already settled into the pattern of university academics, but the transition was much harder for Eric. His entire routine and perspective had changed. There were no more friendly House Masters who made sure that each boy did his lessons, and yet still took an interest in his athletics. Going to college and living with his family, who had been separated for a long time, also raised conflicts. Eric wanted to spend as much time as possible with his mother and Jenny and Ernest, but he also had to study a great deal more than he had done in his final year at Eltham.

Eric's studies were going well in the early winter of 1921, and he felt that he was mastering the routine demanded of a science teacher at the Tientsin Anglo-Chinese College. He had made up his mind to that purpose in 1919, when Professor A.P. Cullen left for China. All he needed to do was to follow in his father's footsteps, complete his university education and then, perhaps, study for ordination in the Scottish Congregational Church. This quiet kind of anonymity, however, was about to be taken away from Eric.

The Liddell family moved that winter to a furnished house at 4 Merchiston Place, about four blocks closer to the giant Craiglockhart athletics facility. A friend who did some cycling and running approached Eric about entering the University Annual Sports which were scheduled for May 28, 1921.

Eric initially said he was too busy to train. During the spring holiday he and four friends impetuously took a five day bicycle expedition to the top of Ben Nevis, a menacing, four-thousand-foot peak 125 miles northwest of Edinburgh. A runner warned Eric that cross-country bicycling developed muscles that would hurt his running. Nevertheless they set out, and by the morning of the third day the five boys were at the peak of the mountain overlooking Loch Linnhe. Two days later, Eric's muscles were so sore that he could not even ride his bicycle to class, much less run in a big track meet.

The soreness passed, however, and Eric entered the Sports. In the first heat of the 100-yard dash he came within inches of beating G.I. Stewart, the clear favorite. Eric then beat Stewart in the final with a 10.4 second performance. In the 220-yard event Stewart ran a 23.4 race and nipped Eric by a foot. The "new luminary" was clearly visible. Stewart wrote that after the 220-yard event he "realised that a new power in Scottish athletics had arrived."

Eric's road to the Olympics had begun. Less than a month later he competed against the best runners from Edinburgh, the University of Glasgow, St. Andrews, which was on the coast just north of the Firth of Forth, and Aberdeen University, which was seventy miles farther up the coast. These four universities engaged annually in the Scottish Inter-University Sports, roughly the equivalent of the U.S. National Collegiate Athletic Association (NCAA) field and track championship.

On June 18, 1921, Eric made it past his qualifying heats without difficulty and then electrified the crowd at St. Andrews by winning the 100-yard and the 220-yard sprints. His time for the 100 yards, 10.6 seconds, was not a world class performance, but his 22.4 second time in the 220-yard race was sensational.

Eric returned to Edinburgh that same evening so as to not miss church services the following day. On Monday morning he was a small sensation at the Heriot Watt campus. More importantly, the university's finest athletics trainer, Tom McKerchar, offered to take him under his wing.

Eric thoughtfully considered what such a decision would do to his life and to his goal of being a missionary in China. He was aware that many athletes lived shallow lives and did not give much to the world after their brief period of athletic glory. Eric prayed and talked the decision over with his mother. Had not the Apostle Paul equated the running of the race with the striving for salvation? Did not God grant him special gifts that He intended to be used? As long as he remembered that the purpose of athletic success is to show forth the glory of God's power, Eric decided that competitive running was a good vehicle for him to serve God.

Later, Eric never doubted that joyful competitive running would honor God and serve his call to be a missionary in China. His family fully supported his commitment to running, though none of them could have predicted how far athletic fame would carry him in his evangelical work at home and abroad.

Tom McKerchar put Eric into a regimen of technical training, overall body development, and muscle adaptation. Tom did not give press interviews, and Eric's modesty always prevented his talking about training details. Both of these things contributed to a charming but totally inaccurate notion that Eric Liddell was a bumbling, badly coached fellow who ran fast because of his faith in God. While Eric did not train with the intensity of today's top Olympic athletes, neither did anyone else in the 1920s. He was coached as scientifically as the best coaching minds knew, and in a world-famous center of scientific and medical innovation.

Eric's coach brought him down to Powderhall, which is about halfway between Edinburgh University and the harbor district, three times a week for training.

Powderhall Stadium lies beside the Water of Leith, a small river that passes through Edinburgh into the Firth of Forth and was used for track events and dog racing in the 1920s. The people ran on the upper track and the dogs chased the rabbit on the lower track, though on separate days.

It was a serious violation of public sensibilities in the 1920s to train in the public parks, even in the knee-length pants and quarter-sleeve shirts used in track meets. Runners in Europe and America therefore had to go to a stadium in street clothes and there change into a running outfit. Street clothes had to be worn for bicycling, too.

Eric thought, at first, that practicing sprinting starts was unnecessary. Starting blocks were not yet used; runners simply dug two little holes in the track with a knife or trowel. Eric liked to run laps, because it gave him a joyful feeling, but he soon accepted the wisdom of practicing starts, relay baton-handoffs, running on the slightly banked turns, stretching his chest for the tape, and keeping his head straight to the front. McKerchar's theory was that muscles had to be softened by massage, and so Eric submitted to having his thighs and calves kneaded by Tom's strong hands after many of his workouts.

Eric also did well in his first year of classes. He scored 94% in inorganic chemistry, and 83% in mathematics, which he enjoyed most. His other subjects were in the range that American college students call "A– to B+", a highly successful transition from a small, specialized boarding school to a front-rank university.

On June 25, 1921, the Scottish Amateur Athletics Association Championship was held at Hampden Park in Glasgow. Eric won the 100-yard sprint in 10.4 seconds and the 220 yards in 22.6 seconds, the latter a Scottish AAA record. This would have been equivalent to an AAU record in the U.S. Eric had thus won the blue-chip events of sprinting in Scotland's three major centers of track and field, in meets sponsored by both major certifying authorities (intercollegiate and AAA), and in both of Scotland's major cities. He was therefore an established national star and was never again the unknown or the dark horse in athletic competition.

Eric later wrote about his early training for those first big meets, when Tom McKerchar was taking him in hand:

> The exercises seemed unimportant at first, but later one
> finds out how useful they have been. He (McKerchar) took

me in hand, pounded me about like a piece of putty, pushed this muscle this way and that muscle the other way, in order, as he said, to get me into shape. Training is not the easiest thing to do. It is liable to become monotonous.

My dinner that June 25, 1921 was no success, in fact it was a nasty failure. The food would not slide down the alimentary canal with any degree of ease, and any that did manage to get down hadn't a dog's chance of being digested. This is the experience that most athletes go through some time in their career, and it makes you ask yourself if it is all worth while.

The Liddells spent the summer of 1921 in a missionary holiday home at Largs. Largs is on the coast, where the Clyde River meets the sea, just a few miles from Helenburgh where James D. Liddell had received the call to China from the Reverend William Blair a quarter-century before. In early July, Eric took the ferry across the North Channel to Belfast for the Triangular International. The meet pitted a track team from England and Wales against national teams from Scotland and Ireland. On July 9, Eric defeated the field, including favored W.A. Hill of England, in the 100-yard sprint with a time of 10.4 seconds. One week later, on Saturday, July 16, he ran at West Kirkbride on the northern tip of the Cumbria lake district in a handicap race. Such races, which were very popular in the 1920s, started slower runners from points in front of the faster athletes, which were calculated from their fastest recorded times, to equalize their abilities. Eric spotted the lake district speedsters two or three yards each in the 100-yard dash and beat them all.

That summer and others at the coast, Eric joined the Life Guard Corps, which had an active component of Christian athletes. The hard sand at the water's edge was great for sprint training, and Eric loved the opportunity to meet youngsters on the beach.

There were also, in that era, youths who came to get drunk and "raise a bit of sand," as the saying went, and Eric developed a wonderful Christian athlete's technique for dealing with the wise guy and the beach bullies.

"You chaps are pretty fast," he would say to the ringleader. "Fact is, people say you're the fastest."

"Right-o," came the braggart's response, "lot faster than any 'Corps' fellow with a funny suit and a whistle."

When the laughter ceased among the bully's admirers, Eric would hand the cap and whistle to one of them. "Just give us a blow, will you? This fellow and I will have a run from here to the jetty."

In the race that followed, Eric invariably left the braggart yards behind, then met him at the finish line with hand extended. "Good race, old fellow, let's run again," he would say. And many a youth then turned to Eric's quiet words on what God's power could do for those who asked for it.

Eric ran to another 100-yard handicap victory at Saltcoats the following week. The summer holiday ended with a humorous incident that happened in the town of Greenock, another Clyde River community.

"Anyone who knows Greenock at all," Eric later reported, "will know that if it is damp at other places it will be pouring there. True to its reputation, it was. This was my first experience of running in really bad weather on a grass track sodden with water. I was in such a hurry to get in after it was all over that I left my large knife for digging my holes out in the rain and it was never seen again."

He somehow missed his ride home, so a motor bicyclist offered to carry him the twenty miles to Largs. Eric sat on a rickety carrier bolted to the rear of the motorbike until a nut worked loose and dropped the carrier and Eric onto the road. The bike owner kept going for about a hundred more yards.

"Picking my pride up and putting it in my pocket," said Eric, "I set off after the motorbike which had halted a hundred yards ahead. The driver was wondering where I had disappeared to, and I was wondering what sort of trick he had been playing on me. With a piece of string we patched things up and I had to sit on the carrier once again for another six miles, feeling certain all the time that the string was getting thinner and thinner and would ere long let me down once again. But, much to my relief, we reached home without further delay."

The Liddells then moved back to Edinburgh. On August 6 the Edinburgh Rangers held their annual meet, which was one of the track events regularly sponsored by big city association football clubs to support athletics and worthy charities. Eric won the 100-yard race in ten seconds flat, spotting the next fastest entry a hefty yard and one-half.

The following Saturday, August 13, he won the 100-yard handicap race in 10.2 seconds. The favorite was Harry Edward, the 1920 bronze medalist in the 100-meter and 200-meter races at the Antwerp Olympics. Harry spotted Eric one yard.

In August, the Glasgow *Herald* summed up Eric's first year of athletic competition:

> Eric H. Liddell . . . is going to be British champion ere long . . . and he might even blossom into an Olympic hero. His success has been phenomenal; in fact it is one of the romances of the amateur path. Unknown four months ago, he today stands in the forecourt of British sprinters.

In the fall of 1921, Eric thought he was going to do his studies, his church work, his running, and spend some time with the family before they returned to China. But some sports organizers found a way to put Edinburgh University on the rugby map by inviting Eric to join the team. The track season was May through July; rugby was played in the fall. Eric loved the game, and, he had been able to work rugby into his schedule at Eltham, so he began practicing with the Edinburgh University XV.

Edinburgh played several rugby clubs in London in November, where A. Leslie Gracie was playing for a club called the Harlequins. By December the two were teamed up again as a quarter-wing combination in a pair of trial matches to select the Scottish national team. In two highly publicized matches—December 3 at Galashiels, a Scottish border town, and Christmas Eve at Edinburgh's Inverleith Stadium—the Gracie-Liddell wing showed its paces. Eric, who had been playing senior rugby for only ninety days, was chosen afterwards as a rugby internationalist. The American football equivalent would be for a college freshman to be selected for the first string All-American NCAA team. The selection of a man with so little experience and from a small boarding school was sensational.

Eric's first taste of international rugby competition was in the famed Stade Colombes at Paris in a tournament with teams from France. The trip from Edinburgh to Paris in the 1920s was as fast as it is today with an overnight train to London, a commuter train to the coast, a steamer to France, and a commuter train onward to Paris. In Eric's debut he played adequately, and the Scottish team pulled out a 3-3 tie against France. The Gracie-Liddell wing did not attract any particular notoriety, because the French team also had a fast wing combination.

In January, Eric settled back into his routine, a kind of structured self-discipline that enabled him to produce so much with his life in such different environments. He usually woke at six or six-thirty in the morning to pray. He then assisted in housekeeping chores, after which he pedaled his bicycle just over a mile to the campus. A typical day included two classes and a science laboratory. He most often used the library for his studies, and only when absolutely necessary did he buy used books at the student exchange. Missionary sons had little money to spend on personal luxuries, but Eric did build up a small collection of science books that he later took to China.

In the mid-afternoon, Eric would cycle southwest to the Craiglockhart playing fields, or almost as far north to the Powderhall stadium. After his workout he had a massage, dressed again in street clothes, and pedaled back to the family house. Supper was a particularly joyful time of togetherness for the Liddells as a family, and Eric was always a welcome guest at other people's tables. After dinner, he typically studied for two or three hours and had a substantial session of prayer and meditation. It was a vigorous, strenuous life, one which prepared him for even greater efforts.

On February 4, Eric made his rugby debut before the home crowd at Edinburgh's Inverleith Stadium. Scotland played to a 9-9 tie against Wales, and even *The Scotsman,* which was known to engage occasionally in some rhetorical favoritism when an Edinburgh sporting hero was involved, found nothing remarkable to say about Eric's play. Three weeks later, again at Inverleith, Eric scored the winning points in a 6-3 win over Ireland. *The Scotsman* was critical of Eric's style and only obliquely mentioned the results on the scoreboard, which suggested to some that the Edinburgh daily was nursing a repressed hope of seeing the Gracie-Liddell wing erupt into instant greatness.

Others evaluated his first season differently. Despite having so little experience, Eric brought speed, sportsmanship, and élan to the Scottish team. As a rugby internationalist, Eric was competing with men who, in some cases, had done little else but train for the sport which he only played seasonally as a student. Three "caps," games played with the national amateur rugby team, with one win and two ties, was outstanding.

Eric's collection of silver cups, trays, plates, wristwatches, and other trophies was beginning to present logistical problems at the Liddell home. His mother was afraid someone might break into the house, and so she insisted on putting the silver cups away in cabinets each night. There was also some controversy over keeping them well shined because in those days trophies were often made from real silver plate or even sterling. Missionary families had their own code of financial ethics as well, and most prizes that Eric brought home ended up, in some manner, supporting another component of missionary life, evangelical work, or aiding someone in need.

The family also moved that spring from Bruntsfield Place to a furnished house at 28 Forbes Road. Eric spent most the spring of 1922 concentrating on his studies. In May, Eric was once again in strict training with Tom McKerchar doing laps, starts, finishing spurts, baton handoffs, and rubdowns. On May 27 he again competed in the Edinburgh University Sports at Craiglockhart. In 1922, however, he was an established star just one year after first gaining national attention at the same meet. While warming up Eric noticed a black athlete, a student from some part of the British Empire, standing off to one side by himself. Eric visited with him in such an unobtrusive manner that it almost escaped everyone's notice. Eric's small acts of kindness were such that they were quite sincere, utterly lacking in personal motive.

In 1922, Eric showed another dimension of his athletic greatness at the University Sport: the ability to produce his best at the big tests. His 100-yard victory in 10.2 seconds tied the meet record, while his winning 21.8-second 220-yard sprint was a native Scottish record. Eric also won the middle-distance 440-yard race in 52.4 seconds, an unusual achievement for a sprinter. That race was his first at that distance in a big meet, and his time would have measured up well at any NCAA track meet in the United States in the 1920s. In addition, the races at Craiglockhart were run on grass, a slower surface than cinder.

Eric had a brilliant summer track season. He won the 100 and 220 at the Scottish Inter-University Sports in June, which paved the way for another showdown against Olympic medalist Harry Edward on July 1 at the Scottish Amateur Athletics Association meet. Eric pulled a muscle severely in a trial heat of another meet, however, and Edward swept to three wins in the Scottish AAA. En route to this meet, Eric showed another trait, remembered vividly by a running mate 45 years later.

The Edinburgh University team occupied two compartments on the train, each compartment holding eight athletes seated four across on facing benches. The train thundered over the Firth of Forth Bridge, then turned east-bound for Aberdeen farther up the coast. At a village station crossing, half a dozen pretty girls waved at the athletes, who noticed how the spring winds whipped the girls' short flapper skirts around their legs.

As the train pulled out, the athletes pulled their heads back inside the train window. The jokes changed from funny to ribald.

"Did you chaps hear the one about the farm lass when the Earl of _____'s touring auto broke down on her father's place?" cried an excited voice.

Eric withdrew into a novel that was tucked in his outside coat pocket. The others gave rapt attention to the joke teller.

"I say, Liddell, get your face out of that book," cried one team-mate. "This joke's capital."

"I've a good part just here," Eric said. He smiled pleasantly and read on.

Suddenly, no one was looking at the joke teller. The atmosphere became awkward, a bit tense.

"What are you doing, Liddell, going holy on us?" taunted the would-be bawdy entertainer.

Eric's serene expression never changed.

"Say fellows," said teammate Neil Campbell, "Tom says the Aberdeen course has some soft spots to beware."

"Bad show, that," answered another.

Sixty-three years later, retired Professor Emeritus Neil Campbell, one of Edinburgh's University's stellar research chemists, put it squarely.

"Eric never made you feel he was being holy or superior," he recalled. "He just showed you the better thing to do, and everyone wanted to do it."

Two weeks later, Eric raced at Powderhall in a locally sponsored meet, and broke a long-standing record, winning the non-standard 150-yard sprint in 15.0 seconds. Two weeks after that, he was back at Greenock, this time with more reliable transportation, and he tied a Scottish native record in the 100-yard handicap race.

His final running performance of 1922 was on August 12 at the Celtic Football Club Athletics Meet in Glasgow. In the non-standard 120-yard sprint, Eric ran from scratch (no handicap) against Harry Edward and won in 12.2 seconds. In the 220-yard race, Eric gave a two-yard handicap to Harry, but won again. The comparison was obvious, and Scottish sportsmen began to talk about the possibility that Eric might go to the Olympic Games of 1924 as a sprinter.

In September, James, Mary, Jenny, and Ernest returned to China. Eric spent all of his time with them as they vacationed at Coldstream on the River Tweed, just prior to their leaving. It was sad parting, because they knew it was probably their last time living together in Scotland.

Rob and Eric then moved to a large house on the east side of George Square, on the Old Campus of Edinburgh University. Today, 56 George Square houses a summer studies program; in the 1920s it was home to the Edinburgh Medical Society. Dr. and Mrs. Lechmere Taylor operated the house for a dozen or so college students who planned ultimately to join the missionary service as doctors, teachers, and ministers. Dr. Taylor had the somewhat less than charming title of "Warden," but the house was a warm, practical environment in which to live. Rob and Eric shared a room, and Eric lived there until his departure for the Olympic Games in June of 1924.

Eric did quite well with his academics while still maintaining his high athletic standards. By utilizing his off-season periods to maximum advantage, he was making grades in the upper 80 and lower 90 percent, and had achieved more advanced levels of scientific courses which required even harder work.

During Christmas, Rob and Eric visited their family at Drymen and Berwick-on-Tweed, and shared in reading long letters from China that told about political instability and social change, yet success for the missionaries.

James and Mary Liddell moved into a large, comfortable house at 6 Taku Road in the French missionary compound at Tientsin in the fall of 1922. Jenny became a student teacher in the kindergarten of the Tientsin British Grammar School. Political uncertainty was the main difficulty in China at the time. In the populous rural zones of the Hopei Province, periodic warlord struggles created much danger for missionaries working the villages. The Kuomintang Party was impressed with social progress in the Soviet Union. They also were encouraged by the Russian withdrawal from Manchuria. The result was that Communist elements were increasingly accepted into Chinese politics.

In January 1923, Eric trained seriously with the Scottish team for the international rugby season. When the series opened at Edinburgh Inverleith Stadium, the Scotsmen whipped France 16-3. The daily newspaper wrote that the "Gracie-Liddell wing was meteoric, even mercurial."

Two Saturdays later, the Scottish team traveled to Cardiff, where they had not been able to beat the Welsh team since 1890. Eric and A.L. were brilliant as the Scots bested the Welshmen 11-8 before a wildly partisan crowd. It seems, however, that Eric and his teammates had a way of projecting sportsmanship beyond themselves. The Welsh team assigned two players to take Eric and A.L. out of the game. They were clipped, tackled by high-low combinations, kicked, and tripped all through the game. Each time an opponent stepped on Eric's fingers, Eric would grin.

But Eric and A.L. got faster and faster. Up in the stands the local fans were drunk, ugly, and anxious to see their heroes smash the two speedy Scots. Howls of rage erupted from the partisan crowd as Eric and A.L. took in three lightning goals in the closing minutes.

When the game ended, the Welsh fans ran onto the field. Ringleaders yelled, "Get the Scots!" An ominous moment ensued. The angry crowd could become violent at any moment, and police entered the field.

"Your chaps played ever so well," said Eric, extending his hand to the ringleader, eyes twinkling. Incredibly, the angry Welshmen picked up Eric on their shoulders and carried the victorious Scots off, while thousands began to cheer. Soon, a victory parade was moving around the track with athletes from both teams riding on the fans' shoulders. "Carry your chaps," said Eric, and they hoisted the Welsh team on their shoulders, too. It was one of those unique sporting events that sets in stark relief the bad behavior of partisan crowds on less happy occasions, and it showed the power of Eric's witness.

On February 24 the Scots defeated Ireland in Dublin 13-3; again, Eric and A.L. were an unstoppable scoring machine. The international season ended April 3 before the home crowd at Inverleith. Both teams played well, but the better-drilled unit from England defeated Scotland 8-6.

Rugby fans did not know at the time that Eric's seventh "cap" match was the end of his international rugby career, although he played the game and taught it to children all his life.

A statistical analysis of his two international seasons is revealing. Scotland finished third in the league in 1922, and second in 1923. Eric's team's record in seven international games was four victories (he missed the final game of the 1922 season because of sickness), two ties, and only one loss. The Scottish team scored 64 points and allowed only 37 for the opponents, and they were widely noted for their sportsmanship. It would not be accurate to say that Eric's personal scoring was the margin of success because rugby is a team game, but it is no exaggeration at all to say that the Liddell-Gracie wing was the scoring weapon that made Scotland successful those two years.

Rob had begun doing work with the Glasgow Students' Evangelical Union that winter. Several students in Glasgow had formed the Evangelical Union the previous year, which included members from all the academic disciplines, student leadership activities, and sports. George H. Morrison was the first president; Robert Dobbie and David P. Thomson were sparkplugs in the campaigns to follow. All the founding members went on the vigorous careers as professors, professionals, ministers, and business leaders.

The Glasgow Students' Evangelical Union organized a tremendous religious revival that influenced the lives of countless thousands. The theological basis was the vigorous, outward-reaching Christianity of the late 1800s encouraged by Henry Drummond and Dwight Moody. The method was the "Manhood Campaign," in which a dozen or so student evangelists went into a town, boarded at the homes of participating volunteers, and conducted three to five public services. Those who attended the GSEU meetings were perpetuating a tradition. It began with a group of student athlete-evangelists from Cambridge University—the "Cambridge Seven"—who had responded in 1884 to the China Inland Mission recruitment campaign. The "Cambridge Seven" had sponsored a hymn-singing rally at Edinburgh's Waverley train station during their memorable visit. In industrial towns they made a particular effort to reach out to factory and shipyard workers, and the new GSEU now renewed this tradition in the spring of 1923.

Their usual method was to put notices on bulletin boards around the campus of Edinburgh University and at churches, advertising a "convener" or featured speaker and a "leader," who served as administrator-organizor of the campaign. In the beginning, the Edinburgh sessions generally brought out several dozen, mostly people who already professed an active faith. D.P. Thomson was assigned, therefore, to put some starch into the GSEU at Edinburgh.

No one denied that the students were sincere religious speakers, but the GSEU needed a drawing card: someone to shock people out of their lethargy and compete with the cinema and the taverns. D.P. talked to Rob, who said he would approach Eric about speaking at an upcoming campaign at Armadale.

No one knows what Rob and Eric said to each other, but it is certain that Eric was shy about public speaking. He did not oppose it. He gloried in his father's preaching and was proud of the work Rob was doing, but he thought of himself simply as a science teacher and an athlete, both in God's service for the China missionary effort, not as an evangelistic speaker.

Armadale is about twenty-five miles west of Edinburgh on the highway to Glasgow, a midlothian industrial city of five thousand people in 1923. Unemployment was high, and working-class men spent a lot of time in the taverns. In that era, before sociologists and psychologists wrote and spoke about social problems, religious leaders were the only social force that concerned themselves with alcoholism, child abandonment, spouse abuse, and all the ugly by-products of economic depression and unemployment.

The GSEU campaign was sputtering in Armadale in March because the working men dismissed the college evangelists as idealistic young men of the privileged social class, people who had nothing in common with their lives. D.P. Thomson hitched a ride on a truck from Glasgow to Edinburgh and came to 56 George Square to put the question squarely to Eric: would he come and be the featured speaker at a rally on April 6?

At first, Eric vacillated. He wanted to be a missionary in China like his father. He admired the Cambridge Seven and their evangelistic zeal, but he treasured his private relationship with God.

Then came a letter from Tientsin. Eric had confided in Jenny his concerns for the future, and she responded in a paraphrase from the Scriptures: "Fear not for I am with thee; be not dismayed for I will guide thee. Isaiah 41, 10. Love, Jenny." Eric talked to Rob and D.P. later in the day.

"All right," said Eric, "I'll come."

Notices were soon put up for a meeting at the Town Hall, since the

GSEU thought a non-religious facility might draw a better crowd. About seventy men arrived for the meeting, which began at 9 P.M. D.P. introduced Eric, who was known to all of them. Eric had no fears about running across the packed cinders or the wet grass, punting the football and smothering an opponent in a tackle, watching for a reaction in a test tube, or cheering up a discouraged companion. But revealing his own inner feelings about his relationship with God before a group of faces was something else.

Eric already had a deep, personal relationship with God that showed in everything he did, but the Armadale experience added a major dimension to his Christian mission: the ability to project his faith to a group. Characteristically, Eric took no credit at all and wrote to D.P. Thomson a letter thanking him for the new opportunity. He gradually overcame his fears and over the next four years spoke to thousands about the love of God in his own quiet, sincere style. As his athletic fame grew, "the new luminary" of Scottish track and field attracted more and more people to the message of salvation.

*O*nce *he got started,* Eric Liddell was tough to beat. As a runner, he was slow getting off the mark. But, as a fan watching the final leg in a relay race at Glasgow in 1925 noted, from there on he was rarely beaten. In that race the first three runners had left Eric a terrific distance to make up, and one of the spectators asked one of the locals in the next seat if Eric would be beaten.

"His heid's no' back yet," he replied, matter-of-factly.

Eric's head then went back, he put on his finishing kick, and won the race.

As an evangelist, the big outcome of Eric's decision to speak at Armadale had nothing to do with his faith or with his athletics. It added the dimension of communicating about God to men in groups with factory workers, sailors, and unemployed workers. He was one of the relatively few evangelists in history who was equally inspiring with persons of all economic and social classes, and in highly contrasting cultures on opposite sides of the world.

Eight days after the Armadale appearance, Eric went to Rutherglen. D.P. Thomson and he addressed about six hundred students the next day in Stonelaw Church to kick off an Easter campaign. No one equated going to an evangelistic meeting with mass conversion. Those in the crowd who wished to give their lives over to the Lord were given an opportunity to talk privately with someone from the organization, and then to be referred to a regular pastor and a church of personal choice.

Eric formally joined the Glasgow Students' Evangelistic Union that same week, on April 20, 1923. Several leaders in the group went on to become high national officials in the Scottish Presbyterian Church.

All of this was important to Eric because his father had studied divinity in Glasgow, was well known in the city, and had been inspired to enter the China missionary service by Henry Drummon and the same men whose work Eric was now extending into the 1920s. This also helps to explain why Eric chose to become associated with an evangelical organization based in Glasgow, which is forty-five miles from Edinburgh, when he had plenty of offers to do religious and charitable work right near his own university.

In May, Eric competed for the third time in the Edinburgh University Sports, and won the 100-, 220-, and 440-yard events for the second year in a row. Coaches in the 1920s thought of the 100-meter and 100-yard events together with the 200-meter and the 220-yard event, and they looked for a different type of runner for the 400-meter/440-yard and 800-meter/880-yard distances. It was unusual for a sprinter to win a middle distance event, but Eric Liddell did it repeatedly. And on this occasion he was even relaxed enough to eat one of Mrs. Taylor's plum puddings before the race!

The next month Eric ran in the Queens Park Football Club Sports in Glasgow, where he did the 100-yard race in 10 seconds flat. He then spent two weeks training intensively for the Inter-Varsity Sport at Craiglockhart on June 16. He delighted the home crowd there by winning the 100 in 10.1 seconds. Although there were several heats, he also was strong enough to win the final in the 220 in 21.6 seconds, a native Scottish record that stood until 1960. Late in the afternoon, he again showed that he was a competitive quarter-miler by winning the 440 in 50.2 seconds, beating J.G. McColl, the reigning champion, by eighteen yards. The quaint, but inaccurate, story that Eric competed in the 1924 Olympic 400-meters as an afterthought is disproved by races such as this one. The 440-yard run is about two-and-one-third yards longer than the 400-meter race and, as a practical rule of thumb, is about two-tenths of a second slower. So by June 1923, over a year before the Paris Olympic Games, Eric was running the quarter-mile in a highly competitive time, even though the slow Craiglockhart grass probably added one full second.

After church services the day following the race, Eric took a bus with D.P. Thomson to Crieff, twenty miles north of the Firth of Forth, where they addressed a large audience at the Morrison's Academy. Eric had earlier written that he felt a lot of joy had been added to his religious life since he began speaking. Eric loved teenagers all his life, and took special concern for them.

The busy pace of his life continued the following Saturday at Glasgow, where he competed in the Scottish Championships at Hampden Park. Several leaders from the Glasgow Students' Evangelistic Union were in the stands to cheer him on as he won the 100-yard sprint and set a meet record with a 22.4 second effort in the 220.

Since college classes were not in session, Eric was approached by the organizers of a benefit event, the Edinburgh Pharmacy Sports at Powderhall. Unable to refuse the organizers of a benefit event, he entered the non-standard 120-yard handicap event, spotted his best rival one yard, and still won the race.

Eric then took a couple of weeks to prepare intensively for what was to be the biggest track meet of his life until the Olympic Games. The British Amateur Athletics Association Championships at Stamford Bridge Stadium in London were scheduled for Friday and Saturday, July 6 and 7. While the qualifying meet for positions on the Olympic squad was not until the following summer, showings at the British AAA would certainly have a large bearing on the selections. Many were speculating whether Eric, who was being called "The Flying Scot" on some sports pages, could beat a Cambridge University sprinter named Harold Abrahams. One newspaper, however, said Eric would be wasting the five pound fare to travel south and race at London.

Tall, genteel, and a jumper as well as a sprinter, Harold Abrahams had served in the army briefly at the end of the war and had finished out of the medals in the 100-meter race at the Antwerp Games in 1920. He became the grand old man of British sports in later years, Olympic Committee mainstay, author, pioneer radio sportscaster, and well-known friend of athletes.

On Friday, Liddell and Abrahams went head-to-head for the first time. Eric had won his first heat in the 220 in 22.4 seconds. In the second heat Harold and he squared off. Abrahams got the better start and appeared to have enough to win, but Eric reached down for a finishing kick and won in a blistering 21.6 time.

A huge crowd gathered under the warm sun on Saturday, and saw Eric win his first heat in the 100-yard sprint in 10.0 seconds, and Harold Abrahams win his first-round heat in 10.2 seconds. Eric ran a scorching 9.8 in his second heat, setting a new British national record. Harold was eliminated, however, in a different second heat. Eric won the final as well, setting still another British record in 9.7 seconds. His time was just one-tenth of a second slower than Charley Paddock's world record time. It was this performance that caused some of the harshest criticisms in England and Scotland when Eric elected not to run the Olympic 100-meter race.

Eric also triumphed in the 220 finals, in 21.6 seconds, and was awarded the Harvey Memorial Cup as best British athletics champion of 1923. He had won six races in twenty-four hours, all in world competitive times! Then the *Bulletin and Scots Pictorial* (usually called the *Daily* or the *Scotsman*) used all the adjectives in the typewriter: world's fastest human, the Scot who would send Paddock packing, the man to finish what Halswelle began (i.e., whipping the Yanks), and more. "The Flying Scot" was, in local sportswriter circles, already the national champion.

The next Saturday Eric proved that his performance was not a fluke, again winning his three events, the last in a way that is one of history's greatest displays of sporting courage. The Triangular International was an awkwardly structured competition in which England and Wales combined to field a national team against a team from Scotland and one from Ireland. Based on relative population and programs for athletes, the meet was a mismatch, but it had great appeal because of historic nationalism. Eric won the 100-yard dash in 10.4, which was inferior to his London performance, and the 220 in 22.6 seconds, again not as good as the Stamford Bridge races.

The 440-yard event was run without benefit of lanes, meaning that the runners could legally cross over in front of one another, although the two-man "boxing in" tactic done by the Americans in 1908 at the London Olympics was prohibited. Eric didn't get a fast start, and fifteen yards out from the gun, J.J. Gillis of the Surrey Athletics Club came driving in for a position at the inside rail and fouled him. A judge immediately declared Gillis the aggressor, as Eric tripped on the low railing and rolled over two times on the grass infield. He mistook the judge's pointed finger and call of "Foul!" to mean that he was disqualified. That is the way his mind worked, even in the heat of national competition.

But a Scottish judge on the infield screamed, "Go on, go on!" Eric got up slowly, caught on to what had happened, and started running again.

The pack was twenty yards in front of him by then, but he caught up with them by the 300-yard point. J.J. Gillis was running well, however, apparently unsure of who had been disqualified, and no one in the crowd really dreamed that Eric might catch him. Spectators were excited that Eric was going to make a "game finish," or even end it "in the medals."

Eric's "heid" went well back, and as the crowd shrieked in disbelief, Eric overhauled Gillis and kicked past him to win by three yards, in a time of 51.2 seconds. He fell down in utter exhaustion, probably from oxygen deprivation. Eric refused an offer of brandy as he got up, saying, "No, thanks, Jimmy, just a drop of strong tea." The English language daily in Tientsin rhapsodized about Eric's great victory, attributing his collapse afterwards to "affected nerves in his head." Just one week later Gillis won the quarter mile in another meet with a 49.8 second performance, which indicates the level at which Eric was competing.

People often questioned Eric after the Stoke-on-Trent "quarter affair," about how he found the resources to come back and win. Perhaps they wanted to hear him say that the injustice of being knocked off the track made him angry at Gillis. Perhaps they wanted to hear that God made a deal with him and helped him run faster. He replied, however, simply, "I don't like to be beaten."

When someone Eric respected inquired one time about the source of his athletic strength in tough races he said, "Why it's the three sevens, you know."

"What are the three sevens?" inquired the friend.

"Seventh book of the New Testament, seventh chapter, seventh verse: 'But every man hath his proper gift of God, one after this manner, and another after that'" (KJV).

Eric would be the first person to say that he was subject to all the hazards every athlete faces, and that God did not give him special favors to win races. On Monday, August 6, he was back at Stamford Bridge for the British Games Meet. He won his first 100-yard heat as expected, but in the second heat he pulled his thigh muscle painfully. Massage would not relieve it, and the muscle cramped so severely that Eric withdrew from the meet after running one more race.

Two days later, Eric forced himself at the Hibernian Football Club Sports benefit in Edinburgh and won the first 100-yard heat in a slow 10.8 seconds. He was beaten badly in the second heat, and in a 100-yard handicap that followed. And on August 11, the best he could make was third place in both sprints at the Celtic Football Club Sports in Glasgow. Eric's values were poignantly revealed by his willingness to run in these races with an injury, for though he hated to lose, as any championship athlete does, he also knew that the sporting benefits would lose big ticket money if he didn't show up to draw the crowd.

In the fall of 1923, Eric played a little rugby with local teams, but concentrated mostly on his studies. He knew that the 1924 track season would take a large part of his time, and he also had his new commitment to evangelical speaking. He therefore had to plan his time in order to receive his Bachelor of Science degree the following summer, so that he could leave for the missions in China.

At the dawn of 1924 the Kuomintang Party was maintaining a dialogue with the Communist Party in China. Mao Tse-tung (Mao Zedong) was gaining power, and Chiang Kai-shek was creating a professional officer corps at the Whampoa Military Academy, under the political guidance of Chou En-lai. James and Mary Liddell looked forward to having Eric join them at the Tientsin Anglo-Chinese College in about seven months. Rob had arrived that winter to take up his medical missionary duties in Fulien, located in South China. Jenny was teaching music at Tientsin, and Ernest was attending the Tientsin British Grammar School.

In France, the Baron Pierre de Coubertin unveiled his First Winter Olympiad, which was held, that one time only, in the same country as that year's summer Olympics. On New Year's Day of 1924, France whipped Scotland by the score of 12-10 in the Rugby internationals. A.L. Gracie played at three-quarter wing, but Eric Liddell was not with them. Eric did play for Edinburgh University in a rugby game against Glasgow University that winter, but he chose to not compete in the international league.

Eric began intensive training for the Olympics with long-distance running through the winter and spring to build up his resistance for Paris's summer heat, which would be difficult for a runner used to the cooler climate of Scotland. He had heard in January that the schedules for the heats and finals at the Olympics had been released, and that the heats of the 100-meter sprint would be on Sunday, July 13. The Baron de Coubertin was concerned that the Games occur with a two-week time frame and not be spread out across the summer as they were at Paris in 1900 and at St. Louis in 1904. Since Monday, July 14 was Bastille Day, which could not be used for sports events in France, the trial heats for the 100 meters and both relay races, the 4 × 100 and the 4 × 400 meters, were scheduled for Sunday.

Eric was disappointed, but those who knew him never doubted nor questioned his decision not to run in those events. It was not a new issue, nor was Eric unique in choosing not to run on Sunday. The practice of honoring the Sabbath by refusing to compete on the Lord's Day was a normal thing among dozens of British and American athletes. In 1900 during the IId Olympiad in Paris, Bastille Day fell on a Saturday, and French officials scheduled trial heats in most of the track and field events for Sunday. Many athletes then decided not to participate, and some who did quarreled bitterly with those who refused. In the 1908 London Games, Forrest Smithson, a theology student from the United States, protested against Sunday trial heats by running the 100-meter hurdles with a Bible in his hand. He attracted attention to his protest by winning the race in world-record time.

It was a simple, uncompromisable decision for Eric; the Fourth Commandment meant precisely what it said. Nevertheless, he received quite a verbal lashing from fans across Scotland and England. "A traitor to Scottish sporting, to all that W. Halswelle stood for," complained one journalist. "A pious lad, no doubt, but more of a publicity seeker in this, we think," ran another.

Eric was deeply hurt. Over and over he studied the Scriptures. "Them that honour me I will honour" (1 Samuel 2:30), came to mind in his prayers again and again. "And if a man also strive for masteries, yet he be not crowned, except he strive lawfully" (2 Timothy 2:5). "I regret that some are hurt over my decision, but there can be no doubt about the Fourth Commandment," was Eric's final answer.

Eric therefore concentrated on training for the 200- and the 400-meter events. Tom McKerchar coached him in every technique known at that time. Both he and Eric were pleased to learn that lanes would be used in the 400-meter race to prevent fouling.

By then Eric was speaking at religious gatherings two or three times per week. He gained confidence each time, and his fame had grown to such an extent that sometimes the crowd was too large for the hall in which they gathered. His athletic fame, especially from the victories at Stamford Bridge and Stoke-on-Trent, had also spread across the

57

Atlantic. Promoters of the Penn Relays in Philadelphia invited Eric to the April event, which was a singular honor because most of the trans-Atlantic athletics competition was between teams from Harvard, Yale, and Princeton in America, and from Oxford and Cambridge in England.

The steamer trip started out badly enough when Eric left his suitcase on the dock. Bad luck continued as the steamer, the *Berengaria,* encountered some ugly spring storms during the crossing. Eric, who had previously sailed halfway around the world, was miserably seasick for six days.

He didn't fare too well at the Relays either. He finished fourth in a special exhibition 100-yard race, though, as loyal sports writers in Scotland pointed out, just thirty inches separated the top four finishers. L.A. Clarke bested Eric by inches in an exhibition 220-yard event. One of the reasons for Eric's weak showing was that it was early in his annual training program cycle; he didn't do well in April at home either.

Eric went to see the inscription over a gate at the University of Pennsylvania. It was already a personal favorite of Eric's, and in 1936 the Baron Coubertin adapted it as the spirit of the Modern Olympic Games.

Chancellor Adolf Hitler was taking control of the 1936 Berlin Olympic Games from the Chairman, Dr. Karl Lewald. He filled the atmosphere with pageantry and polemics that proclaimed his doctrine of Aryan racial supremacy and Nazi political ideology. The aging Baron Coubertin quietly arranged to have a new motto added to the Cirius, Altius, Fortius (Faster, Higher, Stronger) slogan he had euphorically adopted at Paris in 1924. Paraphrased from the University of Pennsylvania motto, it read, "The most important thing in the Olympic Games is not to win but to take part, just as the most important thing in life is not the triumph but the struggle. The essential thing is not to have conquered but to have fought well." When it appeared on the giant signboard in Berlin, Hitler ceased interfering in the Games.* Eric loved to quote the original phrase as he had heard Philip Baker, the British captain in the 1920 Olympics, do so often.

---

* Stan Greenburg, *The Guinness Book of Olympics: Facts and Feats* (Enfield, Middlesex: Guinness Superlatives Ltd., 1985).

Eric's spring season in Scotland began with the Annual University Sports at Craiglockhart. He tied the meet record in the 100-yard sprint in 10.2 seconds, he won the 220-yard race, and then broke the meet record for the 440 in 51.5 seconds, running on spongy, wet grass.

On May 30 and 31, Eric competed at Hampden Park in Glasgow in the Scottish Inter-Varsity Sports. He won the 100 with a 10.2 time, the 220 yards in 22.4 seconds, and the 440 with an excellent 51.4. Two weeks later at the Scottish AAA Championships, he showed he was tuned up for the Olympic Games. His 10.0 second 100-yard dash was a meet record, and he won the 220 in 22.6 and the 440 in 51.2 seconds.

The following week was the qualifying meet in London for the British Olympic team, the meet Eric had been tuning up for all winter and spring. On Friday night, June 21, in a span of just three-and-one-half hours, Eric won two heats in the 220 (22.3 and 21.8 seconds) and two heats in the 440 (51.0 and 49.6 seconds). In Saturday's 220 finals, Eric faced a star-studded field comparable to the kind that would compete at the Paris Games. A.O. Kinsman of South Africa won the event in 21.7 seconds; Eric finished two-and-one-half yards back in second place. New Zealand's Arthur Porritt, who went on to become a medical doctor and five-time Governor General of New Zealand, was third. Porritt wrote forty-six years later in an introduction to the Reverend D.P. Thomson's biography of Eric Liddell how Eric's sportsmanship made an indelible impression on people from all walks of life.

Later that afternoon Eric made a terrific effort in the 440-yard final, winning in 49.6 seconds. This was better than the existing Olympic record for the 400-meter race, which was a full stride shorter. Captain Wyndham Halswelle had run the 440 in 48.4 in 1908, so Eric was well within reach of the British and Scottish native record in the quarter mile.

These results were highly publicized in the *Scotsman,* and Eric returned to Edinburgh in triumph. He also was pleased to learn that he had done well on his qualifying exams for the Bachelor of Science degree, which he believed to be a more important dimension of his missionary preparation than track medals. He was disappointed, in fact, to discover that his grade point average in his final term had fallen during his intensive athletics training. This reflects well on the academic integrity of the Edinburgh University faculty, who didn't give a free ride to an athletics champion and religious hero of the nation.

Eric made a decision on his return that he had been long contemplating. He chose to stay in Scotland a year longer and take the academic work required to become an ordained minister, minus one final term that could be taken on his first furlough. D.P. Thomson, of course, was delighted that Eric would be available for a full year longer to do the public evangelism for the Glasgow Students' Union. Eric also moved that month from the Medical Mission Society house at 56 George Square to the large Georgian mansion at 29 Hope Terrace that housed the Scottish Congregational College. His father and mother approved of his decision, even though it meant that they would not see him for another year.

Scottish track fans may have thought Eric "culdna' lose when his heid's back," but he knew that the competition at the Olympic Games would be the toughest he had ever faced. But Eric believed that the Olympic Games were a superb way to demonstrate the kind of muscular Christianity that made such a difference in thousands of lives, and he was quite willing to accept the challenge.

*P*ierre di Fredi, the Baron Coubertin, wanted to go out in style following the 1924 Olympic Games. He had been the primary influence in the modern Olympic movement since the 1894 international assembly in Paris that first agreed to support the event. The Baron had succeeded in rekindling worldwide interest in the ancient Greek athletic contests, helped in part by "legends" such as the one concocted by his friend, Michel Breal. He told a story about how a Greek soldier, Pheidippides, ran from Marathon to Athens in full armor to bring the news of victory over the invading Persian hordes. "Rejoice, we conquer," he is supposed to have cried before dropping dead on the spot. While Herodotus, the Greek historian, related the incident differently, such grand stories helped the Games get started. Another was the motto Coubertin selected for the Olympics: *Citius, Altius, Fortius!* (Faster, Higher, Stronger)! It was the team motto of a French football (soccer) team, and the Baron adopted it, even though it is Latin, not Greek.

The 1924 Games promised to be the greatest sporting event in the world at that time. The Baron Coubertin was to preside over his final Olympics as the President of the International Olympic Organizing Committee, and forty-four countries were to send over three thousand athletes. For Eric Liddell it would be a magnificent opportunity to project Christianity out to the nations.

The British Olympic team steamed across the Channel during the first week of July, and was quartered at Paris in four hotels. The track and field unit was formidable and was considered to have a serious chance of unseating the highly touted powerhouse from the United States. The Prince of Wales and a large contingent of British nobility came along to inspire the team. Philip Baker, the silver medalist in the 1,500-meter race at Antwerp in 1920, was again Commandant. Harold Abrahams, youngest of three track star brothers, was Captain of the track and field unit. Harold also was a champion long jumper, but he decided to concentrate on the sprints at Paris.

The largest contingent of athletes, nearly four hundred, came from the United States. Some arrived on the ocean liner *S.S. America,* while U.S. Navy athletes came on a battleship. Several nations thought the American effort a bit too lavish. China barely managed to send two athletes, the country's first appearance at the Games.

The roster of gold medal winners at the 1924 Games was indeed impressive. Paavo Nurmi and Vilho Ritola, the "Flying Finns," won two each in distance running. Gertrude Ederle, from New York, won a gold medal for swimming and, just two years later lowered the men's record for crossing the English Channel by 13 percent. Lt. Col. Philip Neame, a graduate of Cheltenham, one of the prep schools influenced by Dr. Thomas Arnold, won a gold medal in team rifle shooting. He had won the Victoria Cross, Britain's highest award for valor, for saving wounded soldiers under incredibly heroic conditions in France during the First World War.

Johnny Weissmuller's three gold medals at Paris made him the king of men's competitive swimming, dethroning "Duke" Kahanamoku. Johnny later created the legendary Tarzan movie role from the Edgar Rice Burroughs novels; the "Duke" became the Sheriff of Honolulu, sporting Hawaii's jaunty flowered shirt with the tail out. Jack Kelly, Sr., and Dr. Benjamin Spock were both gold medal oarsmen at the Paris Games.

At the 1924 Paris Games the athletes exhibited marvelous sportsmanship and broke more records in more sports than in any comparable gathering in the history of the world. At the opening ceremonies, Coubertin unveiled his motto for the Games, "Citius, Altius, Fortius" (Faster, Higher, Stronger). Flocks of pigeons were released, four French bands played, and a two-sport French Olympic athlete receited the Pledge. Captain Philip Christison led the Second Queen's Own Cameron Highlanders, who were sent over from Cologne to inspire the British contingent.

Eric marched with the British team up the Champs Élysées in a moving ceremony at the Tomb of the Unknown Warrior.

The Prince of Wales laid a wreath, and four bagpipers played the dirge, "The Flowers of the Forest," which was written to commemorate the defeat of the Scottish clans by the British forces at the Battle of Flodden Field in 1513.

At the opening ceremonies in the Stade Colombes, the music was much more cheerful. As Eric marched around the track with the British team, he noticed that there would be just one turn in the 400-meter race because of the new, extended 500-meter track the French built after the Seine River had flooded the stadium. The athletes were impressed with the enlarged spectator capacity, but noted warily the high afternoon temperatures, which touched over 110 degrees Fahrenheit several times during those two weeks.

Eric was assigned to stay at the Hotel du Louvre; his roommate was Douglas Lowe, the half-miler. Some other track and field athletes were at the Hotel Moderne nearby on the Rue de la Republique. While some small cabins had been constructed at the Stades Colombes, the British athletes did not use them. They had to jostle for taxi-cabs to get to the stadium. More than one athlete claimed that the Americans always seemed to have enough money to keep the taxis tied up and unavailable to others. Eric certainly didn't have any loose money to spend in Paris, nor did he make critical comments of this kind about any athlete who did.

"Hey Liddell," said a teammate, "wouldn't you like to have the money that's being spent on the American team?"

"No . . . no," said Eric thoughtfully. "A lot of money's not the thing. Just the athletics, you know."

"Athletics, rot," retorted the other. "It's a shame how the Americans have ruined the Games. Professionals, they are, not athletes."

"I'm not fond of all the fuss and feathers," said Eric, "but their athletes are not to blame. Splendid fellows, you know, Horatio Fitch, Jackson Scholz, top-drawer chaps."

Captain Cristison, now Brigadier Sir Philip Cristison, Retired, commanded the British military bagpiper unit sent to Paris "to pipe on the lads a bit." Forty-one years later, he reminisced, "There was a lot of talk against the Americans for spending too much, for being too garish. But you never heard it from Eric. He was a friend of every athlete."

On Friday, July 4, the American athletes participated in their own patriotic ceremonies, and on Saturday both the British and the

American track and field units held workouts. The two teams, plus the British Empire and Commonwealth countries, contained just about all the track and field power of the world, except for the "Flying Finns," Nurmi and Ritola. Germany sent some fine athletes, but they felt they had been insulted by the French Olympic Committee when they arrived and so left before the Games began.

On Sunday, the trial heats were held for the 100-meter event. Eric participated instead in services at the Scots Kirk (Church). Not one athlete criticized him for his decision. Eric actually talked about the power of faith. Harold Abrahams, whose 10.6 was the fastest qualifying time, was the only British team member to make it to the finals. His coach, Sam Mussabini, was the guiding force of the Polytechnic Harriers, and had already trained Willie Applegarth, the bronze medalist in the 200 meters at Stockholm (1912), and Harry Edward, the 200-meter bronze medalist at Antwerp (1920).

Eric was present in the stadium on Monday, July 7, for the 100-meter finals. Four Americans were in the field, including the favorite, Charley Paddock, who had run the 100-yard sprint, which is a bit longer than the 100 meters, in 10.2 seconds in 1921. Early in 1924 Paddock clocked in a world-record 10.4 seconds for the 100-meters, and he still held the Olympic mark of 10.8 which he set at the Antwerp Games. Jackson Scholz from the University of Missouri was Paddock's equal, and each of the other Americans, Chester Bowman and Loren Murchison, could certainly be in the race on the right day. Art Porritt of New Zealand, the sixth starter, was not considered to have much of a chance for a medal.

The tall, powerful Abrahams ran his best race ever that day. He made a great start and held the lead all the way, beating Scholz by two feet in an Olympic-record 10.6 time. Art Porritt nipped Bowman for the bronze medal, so the British fans celebrated a 1-3 finish. Reginald Walker of South Africa, another runner trained by Sam Mussabini, had been the only British Empire runner to win the 100-meter race (1908); no runner wearing the Union Jack on his shirt had done it until Abrahams.

The British team was also excited about their prospects on Tuesday, July 8. Charley Paddock was so disconsolate over his surprising fifth-place showing (10.9 seconds) in the 100-meters that he planned to drop out of the 200-meters race. His friends Maurice Chevalier, Douglas Fairbanks, and Mary Pickford took him out that night to cheer him up.

Mary Pickford told him, "If you believe in yourself, you will win tomorrow."

Eric won his first qualifying 200-meter heat in 22.2 seconds, and made it to the semi-finals by placing second in his next heat. Harold Abrahams won both of his trial heats, and Charley Paddock won a heat in fine style. The runners noticed that the times were slower because the cinders in the freshly laid track were not packed tightly and the heat was extreme.

On Wednesday, Abrahams barely qualified for the finals with a third-place finish in the semi-final. Eric's semi-final included Charley Paddock, who also held the world record in the 200 with 20.8 seconds set in 1922. Charley won the heat in 21.8, nipping Eric by one-tenth of a second. The final was set: two Britons would run against four Americans.

Bayes M. Norton was in the first lane; Harold Abrahams in lane two; lane three, G.L. Hill; lane four, Jackson Scholz; lane five, Eric Liddell; and on the outside, the reigning champion, Charley Paddock. Paddock got a great start and led most of the way until Jackson Scholz nipped him at the tape. Scholz's 21.6 seconds was a new Olympic record. Eric put on a fast finish and moved from a weak fifth place to edge Hill and Norton for the bronze medal.

Eric was the first Scot to medal in the 200 meters and the first to medal in any Olympic event since Halswelle in 1908. The *Scotsman* ran a story titled "Thrilling Olympic Finishes." It said, "As usual, Liddell did not start too well, but made a wonderfully fast finish."

Douglas Lowe had won the 800-meter race for the British team on Tuesday, so British team spirits were very high going into the 400-meter event. During the early afternoon on Thursday, July 10, Eric won his first heat comfortably in 50.2 seconds. His teammate, Guy Butler, the silver medalist at Antwerp, ran the same trial in great pain, his sprained thigh muscle so heavily taped that he could not even crouch down for the start. He survived the first round heat, however, and both Guy and Eric felt optimistic about their chances.

Eric was nipped out for first place by Adrian Paulen from the Netherlands in his second heat. Paulen, who later became President of the International Amateur Athletics Federation, the world umbrella organization that controls amateur track and field, registered 49.0 seconds. In a later heat, Joseph Imbach from Switzerland broke the

Olympic record with a stupendous 48.0 seconds performance. Eric knew he would have to improve his best-ever time by over a full second in order to win the event.

The records continued to fall on Friday afternoon. Horatio Fitch beat Guy Butler in their third heat in an Olympic-record 47.8 seconds. The injured Butler finished in 48.0, breaking Halswelle's British record of 48.4, set in 1908. Eric won his third heat in 48.4 seconds, a time that would have been good enough for a new Olympic record just a few hours before, but by then was just in the middle of the pack. Eric considered that race to be his personal best performance in any competition. He beat Imbach and J.C. Taylor, who had qualified first at the U.S. Olympic trials, besting Horatio Fitch with a 48.1 performance.

The stage was set for the 6:30 P.M. finals, just two-and-one-half hours after Eric's third heat. No one but Eric really thought he would finish in the medals.

As the six finalists were called to the line, Eric opened a scrap of paper that someone had handed him at the Hotel Moderne when they were gathering up the team for the ride to the stadium. It read, "In the old book it says, 'He that honours me I will honour.' Wishing you the best of success always." And it was signed by one of the trainers who helped Tom McKerchar give Eric his rubdowns.

"The Flying Scot" dug two little holes in the track and walked across the line of runners shaking hands. Captain Christison lined his Cameron Highlanders in formation on the infield grass and said to them, "Come on, let's strike up." There was no rule against it, and so they played a few bars of "Scotland the Brave."

In lane one was Canada's D.M. Johnson; Guy Butler, still with his thigh taped, was in lane two; Joseph Imbach drew lane three; J.C. Taylor, lane four; Horatio Fitch, lane five; and Eric, the least experienced quarter-miler there, was in lane six, staggered in front of the rest to compensate for the one curve in the track. He, therefore, would least be able to judge his position against the other runners, but he had a different plan in mind.

There was no concern about "boxing in," because of the lane dividers. The gun cracked, and Eric took off at his fastest sprint pace. Spectators who knew the runners saw immediately what he was doing. They also knew that he had just run his own fastest 400 about two hours before in temperatures that were nothing like the breezy climes of Scotland.

At the halfway mark Eric was unofficially clocked at 22.2, a time which would have won many a 200-meter heat. Even his loyal supporters knew he could not hold such a pace, and Horatio Fitch closed up on him as they entered the one curve in the course. Taylor and then Imbach both lurched forward onto the track, caught themselves, and resumed running, but they were out of the race. Eric's head went back, and incredibly, he began to open up the distance on Fitch—three meters, then four, and then five. His head was tipped back just a bit more than Fitch's head, and his form was superb. He thrust out his chest and broke the tape, five meters ahead.

Eight or ten steps farther he pulled up, turned, and clasped Horatio's hand. He walked back a few steps and gave a handshake and a kind word to the two who had fallen, and special praise to his courageous teammate Guy Butler, the bronze medalist. Eric waved a bit at the wildly demonstrative British crowd in the bleachers, turned to pick up his jacket, and started walking away. He paused briefly for the announcement, first that his 47.6 seconds time was an Olympic record, the fourth in two days. Then, another annoucement was made: his time was a world record, since Ted Meredith's 47.4 in 1916 was done at a different distance, 440 yards, and without lane dividers.

Eric left the stadium immediately after the playing of "God Save the King." The winners didn't stand on boxes to be draped with medals in 1924; they were mailed to the winners several weeks after the Games. So Eric went to his hotel to rest and the next day gave some press interviews and worked on his talk for the Sunday services at the Scots Kirk.

The *Scotsman* pulled out the stops the next day: "The greatest achievement in the Olympic Games so far has been accomplished by a Scotsman. . . . This is the crowning distinction of Liddell's great career on the track, and no more modest or unaffected world champion could be desired." The headline was "Liddell's Great Olympic Triumph: World Record Broken!" Harold Abrahams gave the one accurate opinion about Eric's style, since dogmatic sports writers of the day often felt constrained to equate Eric's arm action and head angle with some kind of coaching failure; "People may shout their heads off about his 'appalling style.' Well, let them; he gets there," said Abrahams. Ted Meredith, the United States' great quarter-miler whose world record Eric had just broken, watched the race and later commented, "Liddell is the greatest quarter-miler ever seen."

Eric was asked, of course, many questions by reporters. He was too modest to give out biographical details, and so all sorts of errors went into the newspapers and then into even the best books about the Olympic Games. It was variously written that he was a divinity student, that he lived in Glasgow, that he was short ("bandy-legged," said one writer who failed to note that Eric was the same height as two of the other finalists), and that he had just switched over to the 400-meter race to spite the authorities.

Eric's wit superbly handled questions about the possible influence of the Cameron Highlanders' short battle tune just before the starting gun. "I suspect," said Eric, "either General Kentish or Philip Baker laid a dark plot to terrify the others."

The reporters also wanted to know how he kept up the pace in the second half. They had obviously been tipped off that he might make a religious connection, some inference of divine assistance. "The secret of my success over the 400 meters," recorded a Scottish reporter, "is that I run the first 200 meters as hard as I can. Then, for the second 200 meters, with God's help, I run harder."

Eric had become a famous world-class athlete, not merely a Scottish national figure. The Olympic Games projected him at his best, showing the things he would deny in God's name and the things he would strive to do to show God's power. He was Coubertin's perfect amateur, as it was written in the rules of the International Olympic Organizing Committee. But he was not a gawkish, amateurish man who ran well because of some momentary religious inspiration. He was a magnificently coached athlete who had been well trained and who had paid the price of hard training, while keeping up studies and religious speaking engagements. In a sophisticated environment of nobles, movie stars, world record holders, generals, press, and government officials, he had shown himself to be the friend of everyone, to be more concerned about the two runners who fell down than about his own time at the finish line.

Eric Liddell kept his sense of humor and his basic orientation as a man called upon to serve God by serving others all his life. Pride could have ensnared him after his victory on July 11, 1924. He was *Citius, Altius, Fortius* in Paris; but he was first and always God's joyful runner.

*F*rom July 11, 1924, until just under a year later, Eric Liddell lived an inspired, highly public life. He began his studies for a divinity degree and delivered over one hundred public addresses before audiences of all sizes in the campaign for Christian enlistment. He defended his Olympic, British, and Scottish national running titles at championship meets, and also ran invitational meets to help draw out a good crowd for the sponsors.

After the parades and ceremonies to honor Bastille Day in Paris, the British Olympic team crossed the English Channel by steamer. They received a tumultuous welcome at Victoria Station in London, and Eric was carried on the shoulders of waiting fans to the overnight train for Edinburgh. At Waverley Station, a thunderous crowd of students and townspeople greeted him, and escorted him to his quarters at 29 Hope Terrace.

Just a few days later, on July 17, Eric was at Edinburgh University's McEwan Hall to receive his bachelor of science degree. Many distinguished leaders of the realm were there to be awarded honorary doctor's degrees: Lord Macmillan, the publisher; Sir Frederick Whyte; Professor George M. Trevelyan, author of the multi-volume history of Britain; political economist Mrs. Sidney Webb; and the editor of *Punch,* Sir Owen Seaman. The hundreds of students applauded politely as they received their diplomas and hoods from the Vice-Chancellor, Sir Alfred Ewing.

Unknown to Eric, the two graduation marshals, each a professor of Greek classics, had planned a special honor for the school's graduating Olympian. In ancient Greece, Olympic event winners were presented a crown made of entwined olive leaves. Laurel leaves were used at the Pythian Games, pine garlands were awarded at the biennial Isthmian Games of Corinth, and wild celery leaves were given at the biennial Nemean Games. Olive leaves do not grow in Edinburgh, but the two professors approached the keeper of the Royal Botanical Gardens to see what he could do. The keeper offered them oleaster sprigs, a garden derivative of the olive plant.

They also needed a Pindaric ode to give Eric's welcome the right symbolism. In the 5th century B.C. Pindar had been commissioned to honor the athletic champions at Olympia, and other Greek games, with odes intended to be sung in a choral procession in the victor's home city. The words of one, among others, have survived to this day:

> Creatures of a day. . . . What is someone? What is no one?
> Man is merely a shadow's dream . . . But when God-given
> glory comes upon him in victory . . . A bright light shines
> upon us and our life is sweet . . . When the end comes, the
> loss of flame brings darkness . . . But his glory is bright
> forever.

Professor Mair agreed to create a Pindaric gem, one which even an undergraduate student might translate with a bit of help.

It was finally time to present the bachelor's degrees at McEwan Hall. The marshal called out each name as the students ascended the stage. The crowd remained silent in those days before microphones and loudspeaker systems.

"The Bachelor of Science degree, Mr. Eric Henry Liddell," the marshal said as Eric ascended the stage. The crowd leaped to their feet and suddenly the august academic affair became something between a track meet and a religious rally. Minute after minute, the cheers thundered on, as spontaneously joyful as the heart of the man for whom they were intended. The distinguished officials on stage maintained a discreet demeanor, though here and there a tear was seen. Finally, Sir Alfred called for silence, and after several more rounds of cheering, the boisterous crowd settled down.

Mixing Eric's recent 400-meter victory at Paris with the recently completed graduation examinations in a dreadful pun, Sir Alfred began:

"Mr. Liddell, you have shown that none can pass you but the

examiner. In the ancient Olympic tests the victor was crowned with wild olive by the High Priest of Zeus, and a poem written in his honor was presented to him. A Vice-Chancellor is no High Priest, but he speaks and acts for the University; and in the name of the University, which is proud of you, and to which you have brought fresh honor, I present you with this epigram in Greek, composed by Professor Mair, and place upon your head this chaplet of wild olive." Sir Alfred placed the oleaster wreath on Eric's head, and the crowd erupted wildly for several more minutes. While Eric grinned, Professor Mair read the Pindaric gem:

> Happy the man who the wreathed games essaying
> Returns with laurelled brow,
> Thrice happy victory thou, such speed displaying
> As none hath showed till now;
> We joy, and Alma Mater, for they merit
> Proffers to thee this crown:
> Take it, Olympic Victor. While you wear it
> May Heaven never frown.

Somehow, the other students received their diplomas, but the celebration had hardly begun. Eric emerged from a side door with the other new graduates, the olive garland still adorning his head. The leaves slightly obscured Eric's receding hairline in front, which his mother, far away in China, jokingly attributed to the many showers Eric took after his athletic workouts. Unfortunately, none of his family witnessed Eric's Olympic triumph or the honors that followed. His sister, Jenny, did attend a celebration in Eric's honor at Edinburgh University, however, in 1982 to commemorate the Eric Liddell Memorial Gymnasium for handicapped people.

The students carried him out from McEwan Hall, northward into the Bristo Place, past the Heriot Watt College, and then to St. Giles Cathedral. The street was filled with men and women, mostly students, as the procession wended its way into the "Westminster Abbey" of Scotland, the birthplace of the Presbyterian Church. At St. Giles, the crowd filled the street and backed onto the terrace of the City Chambers. They shouted for Eric to make a speech. He thought quickly about the famous old gate through which he had just been carried, and his mind raced to another university far away. The crowd fell silent.

"Over the gate at Pennsylvania University," said Eric, his words carrying to perhaps two or three hundred people, "there is a motto. It reads, 'In the dust of defeat as well as in the laurels of victory there is a glory to be found if one has done his best.' There are many men and women who have done their best, but who have not succeeded in gaining the laurels of victory. To them, as much honour is due as to those who have received these laurels."

They attended the traditional service of thanksgiving, and Eric was next driven to University Union for the Graduation Luncheon. All the top officials of Edinburgh and of the university were present, and it was outside the normal custom for the recipient of a bachelor's degree to be a special honoree, seated and toasted repeatedly with the distinguished recipients of the honorary doctorates. Mrs. Sidney Webb responded to the toasts on behalf of all the honorees, and then Professor Richard Lodge, a noted historian, gave a special tribute to Eric.

Professor Lodge first pointed out that Edinburgh, which was considered a modern Athens in the cultural sense, was seeing an unusual amount of Greek spirit and influence that day. He then got quite a laugh by pointing out that even a bachelor of science graduate should have no difficulty in translating his fancy Greek epigram, since the recipient was both "a Liddell and a Scot," a reference to the popular *Liddell and Scott Greek-English Dictionary.*

Eric rose to speak, and the large banquet hall fell silent.

"I ask you to remember today that I suffer from a certain defect of constitution," he said. Surprised looks registered on his listeners' faces. "I am a short-distance runner, a sprinter, because I suffer from short-windedness, and therefore I will not detain you for long." The audience laughed and clapped.

"The papers have told you that my form, my action, is extremely bad," Eric continued. "But this condition can probably be traced to my forefathers. As we all know in Scotland, the Borderers used to visit England now and then, and escape back as quickly as possible. It was no doubt the practice of my forefathers to do this," said Eric, referring to the cross-border raids that the English called sheep stealing. "The speed with which my forefathers returned from England seems to have been handed down in my family from generation to generation. They had to get back as best they could, and one did not look for correct action. So this probably explains my own running action."

The irony of this modest humor is that later generations of sports experts, less dogmatically committed to defining correct form as the style used by the champions of their own day, expressed the opinion that Eric drew his best muscle power into his running with his unorthodox style.

"I would like to close by reminding us all that a man is composed of three parts—body, mind, and soul—and it is only when we teach each part in such a way as not to overstress it at the expense of the others, but give to each what it is entitled to, that we will get the best and the truest graduates from the University. When we realize that we have not only to store the mind with knowledge, but also to educate the body for the strenuous life that it must go through, we will pass down graduates who are really worthy to take their place in any field of life." Thomas Arnold would have loved this explicit exposition of his human development philosophy.

As the Graduation Luncheon ended, a large contingent of University "Blues," lettermen in American terms, pulled up at the front entrance of Union Hall with a hero's chariot. It was a carriage with spoked wheels, ribbons in the national and university colors, and muscular athletes pulling ropes in place of the draft horses. Sir Alfred Ewing, the Vice-Chancellor, and Eric entered the carriage, and the parade began. The unusual procession wended its way though the business hour traffic on Princess Street past the Sir Walter Scott Monument, and up the Royal Mile where the monarchs of Scotland's history had walked or ridden for hundreds of years. Then the athlete "horses" doubled back to the Vice-Chancellor's house where tea was served to Eric and the athletes, who wore suits with vests on the hot July day. The Vice-Chancellor observed that he had never basked in so much reflected glory.

On Friday about one-hundred-and-twenty distinguished citizens who so admired Eric's leadership and personal example that they had sent him a congratulatory telegram at Paris, all came together for a dinner in Eric's honor at Mackie's Dining Salon. Lord Sands, a noted theologian and jurist, was the keynote speaker. He pointed out how the quarter-mile was a particularly tough race. And with pride he noted that only two Scots, Wyndham Halswelle and Eric Liddell, had won Olympic gold medals, and that each won them in the quarter-mile. And, he noted, their friend Eric Liddell was about to enter a race that was more strenuous and harder than the quarter-mile. The comparison with

Halswelle, of course, was tough for Eric to hear, because Halswelle had been killed by a German infantry sniper in France.

"I thank you for your kind words," said Eric, "but I must remind you that running is not my career. I am training to be a missionary in China, and I will now devote all my spare time to that training until I go out East to evangelistic work among the young men in China. I would like to have your help and your sympathy in this work."

But racing must have been on his mind, for he went straight to the Waverley Station and took the night train to London. A special relays meet had been set up at Stamford Bridge to take advantage of the large concentration of U.S. and British Olympic athletes who were still available to compete. A crowd of thousands turned out. A mile-relay event was staged, each runner doing a quarter mile, the times of which could be compared with the recent Olympic results in the slightly shorter 400-meter four-man relay race. The Americans won the event in Paris in a time that tied the world record set by an earlier American team, and the Swedes were a close second over the British team. Eric's times in the 400-meter races, if substituted for Britain's slowest man in the 4 × 400 meter unit, would have resulted in a gold medal and world record for Britain. Eric had not run in the event because the heats were on Sunday.

But times added together on paper are not the same as times registered on a track, and Eric had something to prove at Stamford Bridge. Britain's George Renwick of the 4 × 400 meter bronze medal unit at Paris dropped off the team and Eric was added as the anchor man. The other three were the same: Edward J. Toms, Richard N. Ripley, and Guy Butler.

The United States also added some speed to its unit: Bill Stevenson, from the gold medal foursome at Paris remained, and Commodore S. Cochrane, Alan Helffrich, and J. Oliver McDonald were replaced by E.C. Wilson, R.A. Robertson, and Horatio M. Fitch, the silver medalist in the 400-meter race against Eric at Paris. Horatio's speed gave a margin of improvement to the American unit about equal to what Eric's presence was for the British unit. Bill Stevenson was another of the 1924 Olympics legendary figures. He enlisted for combat as a U.S. Marine in World War I, was a Rhodes Scholar out of Princeton to Oxford and later became President of Oberlin College in Ohio (1946-1959), and was President John F. Kennedy's Ambassador to the Philippines (1961-1964). His World War II service would briefly touch Eric's family in 1945.

74

The race was held on Saturday, July 19. After the first three laps, the American runners had given Horatio Fitch a six-yard lead over Eric Liddell. The Flying Scot had the crowd with him, but also was coming off four days of banquets and very little practice. He didn't make up any ground in the first 100 yards. At the mid-point in the race, Eric made up about two yards on Fitch. Then, near the 300-yard point, "his heid went back" and he put on the strongest finishing sprint of his career. With fifty yards to go he pulled even, then tore past his rival and won the race with a four-yard lead. The crowd went utterly wild. Eric had gained a full ten yards on the world's fastest 4 × 400 meter relay team.

Eric went back to Edinburgh, and the newspapers were filled with photographs of him and stories about his exploits. On Friday, July 25, he was the guest of honor at another banquet, a luncheon given by municipal officials. It certainly did not hurt Eric's standing that he had helped whip the American mile relay team, showing what might have been at Paris had not the heats in the 4 × 400 meters been on Sunday. His critics finally had the matter of his not running sorted out correctly, and by then the press was full of admiration for the moral stand Eric had taken.

At the luncheon, Eric was praised for his running and his commitment to his principles. He also was given a gold watch, engraved, from the City of Edinburgh. In his response, he credited trainer Tom McKerchar with taking him in hand in 1921 when he was a novice, and with showing him how to stretch out his paces from the sprints to the 400-meters/440-yards events.

Eric was back on the track the next day, braving the rainy weather at Greenock, where the Glenpark Harriers were sponsoring a Canada-Scotland meet. Canada's Olympic sprinter, Cyril Coaffe, won the 100-yard event; Eric came in third. He then won the 440-yard race in 51.2 seconds on a sopping wet track and anchored the Scots to a victory in the mile-medley relay. The following Saturday he was in Glasgow for the Rangers Football Club Sports where he beat the field in a 440-yard handicap with a time of 49.6 seconds.

Eric was busy all summer running in meets and charity events, speaking to groups about his faith, and preparing to enter the Scottish Congregational College. It is hard to estimate the impact he had on his countrymen, especially young people. One of those whom he inspired was Peter Marshall, who hung on every achievement and every word of

Eric Liddell. That summer Peter, a young student at the time, was working at a temporary job in Bamburgh, a British village on the North Sea coast some sixteen miles below the Scottish border. He never forgot the influence of Eric Liddell on his life. Peter had a vision at Bamburgh, after which he knew that he would devote his life to God's service. He dreamed of becoming a missionary in China like Eric, and he wrote to the London Missionary Society and to Dr. Hughes at the Congregational College. But Peter was rejected by both the College and the China missionary service. Following Eric's words at a rally about God's way of hiding triumphs under tragedies, Peter came to America. He graduated from Atlanta's Columbia Theological Seminary and went on to a pastoral career that culminated as chaplain to the U.S. Senate, becoming one of America's most respected religious leaders. He never forgot the influence of Eric Liddell on his life.

Another student in Edinburgh was inspired that fall to apply for the China missionary service. Miss Annie Buchan from Peterhead, on the northeast coast of Scotland, had completed her training at the Missionary College and was finishing up her work at the missionary medical training center on Inverleith Terrace. She planned to join Rob Liddell on the staff of the little hospital in Siaochang, where she later met "Dr. Rob's" famous brother.

Another young woman who was influenced by Eric was Miss Elsa McKechnie, a student at the George Watson's Ladies' College. She was attracted to Eric because of her disillusionment with the distance between the preaching and the practices of many of the adults around her. Eric Liddell struck her as an adult who was sincere, moral, Christian, and believable. So, at the age of fourteen, Elsa McKechnie formed an Eric Liddell Club. The members agreed to believe in and to practice the things that Eric showed in his life. They often went to hear Eric speak at the Morningside Congregational Church as well. On one occasion, there was an overflow crowd at the church, but when Elsa and her girls were told that they should go to another church nearby to hear one of the other GSEU speakers, Elsa said, "We came to hear Mr. Liddell, and we are going to stay here." And they did.

On August 5, 1924 the West of Scotland Harriers sponsored an invitational meet at Ibrox. Eric won the 300-yard event in 32.0 seconds. The following Saturday he was at Galashiels, a Scottish town just above the English border. They ran in pouring rain and Eric gave a huge handicap in the 440-yard race, but he won again, in 54.0 seconds.

In September the Glasgow Students' Evangelical Union opened a campaign at Ardrossan, on the coast where Eric had vacationed with his family, and not far from where his father received the missionary call. "The students," reported a local newspaper columnist, "are a group of eager, alert, bustling, athletic and well-developed young men, full of enthusiasm and the strength of their own convictions, talking in a manner confident and inspiring, to people many years their seniors, yet with a wonderful power of appeal and magnetic attraction. Far from being kill-joys or mik-sops, these lads represent all that is manly and upright."

The September campaigns ended up at Kilmarnock, a town of forty thousand to the southwest of Glasgow. The GSEU men gave six public talks per day, working in several of the city's Protestant churches. Eric drew crowds in excess of a thousand. A sister campaign was conducted in Glasgow, where Eric made several successful talks from the pulpit of the Dundas Street Congregational Church, the place at which his father had been ordained. Several times the crowd was so large that they filled another church besides the one announced for the meeting. They also made presentations at high schools, sporting clubs, and the local YMCA.

Eric's name was a powerful drawing card at any rally, but he was learning that an itinerant religious crusader must also take a concern for the business elements of evangelism. They needed to schedule halls, collect and account for the money, and convince many of the local ministers and school headmasters of the value of an enthusiastic team of muscular Christians coming in for a campaign. There were also difficult social issues to address, such as drinking, smoking, and gambling. Religious opponents of the social vices customarily portrayed them as moral evils, citing biblical precedents. Eric tried, however, to draw on examples from chemistry, sports, and social experience whenever possible, rather than to throw religious platitudes at his listeners.

Not all Scots wanted Eric's company for selfless, noble purposes. One celebrity collector invited Eric to a party, then notified friends that "the world famous Olympian Liddell would be dropping by." Eric arrived for the chic affair, swathed in towels. "Tell the host it's 'Liddell, Knight of the Bath' you're announcing," he told the astonished butler. If the host didn't get the message, the guests did.

During that fall, Eric became Secretary and Treasurer of the Edinburgh Auxiliary of the GSEU. The following February he was made President. These positions were excellent training for missionary service. Also by that time he was learning how to deal with fame. People would often stop him as he pedaled his bicycle around Edinburgh and expect him to say something inspiring and sign an autograph.

Eric participated in three evangelistic campaigns during the following spring. The first was Barrhead, near Glasgow. One young girl was so overwhelmed by Eric's presentations that she wrote a poem to the local newspaper.

> To Barrhead comes a gallant man,
>   Who in Olympic races ran,
> Gained first prize, and led the van—
>   Victorious Eric Liddell!
>
> He comes a nobler race to run,
>   To strive for Master's prize—'Well done,'
> Which he'll deserve when duly won—
>   Undaunted Eric Liddell!
>
> True soldier of the Cross thou art.
>   To fight 'gainst wrong, and take the part
> Of sinners struck by Satan's dart—
>   Great-hearted Eric Liddell!

In April 1925, Eric participated in an invitational campaign at the London YMCA that was aimed at working men in the big city. Unemployment and social unrest were common then, and the cynical men of the city were not awed by wholesome college athletes. Eric stood up and told them that he was opposed to drinking alcoholic beverages and to smoking. In those days, social events were often called "smokers" in order to draw a large crowd. Eric didn't preach that they were doomed to lose salvation if they indulged in those things, simply that they were bad health risks. One by one, the cigarettes went out, and at the finish, men who had jeered at other evangelists cheered loudly for Eric.

The London campaign concluded with two tremendously successful church services, attended equally by men and women. YMCA and church officials reported a great upsurge in religious interest, in attendance at events, and some reduction in public drunkenness following the campaign. Just after that came the great Young Life Campaign in Edinburgh, which was so large that it received daily press coverage and is still referred to today when discussing great rallies. The *Scotsman* gave this report, referring to Eric and D.P. Thomson who were the featured speakers: "Both men rely not upon emotional fervour at the expense of reason, but on the direct challenge both to mind and heart of intelligent and robust young manhood . . . one is frequently reminded . . . of Henry Drummond forty years ago in his cooperation with [Dwight] Moody."

A week later Eric addressed a crowd of one thousand women and two hundred men at St. George's United Free Church (Edinburgh):

> Young, inexperienced, and without eloquence, we have come before you because we feel that we have a message for you. . . . We feel youth has an appeal to youth, and we want to give you our experience. We are placing before you during these few days the thing we have found to be best. We are setting before you one who is worthy of all our devotion—Christ. He is the Saviour for the young as well as the old, and He is the one who can bring out what is best in us. . . .
>
> Are you living up to the standards of Jesus Christ? We are looking for men and women who are willing to answer the challenge Christ is sending out. . . . Have you sought a leader in everyday life? In Jesus Christ you will find a leader worthy of your devotion and mine. I looked for one I could admire, and I found Christ. I am a debtor, and no wonder I am a debtor, for He has given me a message which can only be experienced. If this audience was out-and-out for Christ, the whole of Edinburgh would be changed. If the whole of this audience was out for Christ, it would go far past Edinburgh and through all Scotland. The last time Edinburgh was swept, all Scotland was flooded. What are you going to do tonight?

For the final night of the Young Life Campaign, Eric addressed thousands at Usher Hall, then an overflow crowd at the Lothian Road Union Free Church, and then an overflow crowd at St. Cuthbert's. He warned against mere emotionalism and called for hundreds of individual commitments.

On May 20, 1925, Eric appeared for the fifth time in Edinburgh University Sports, at Craiglockhart. His presence probably doubled the crowd. That spring he was in top form early. On the grass track he won the 100-yard sprint, the 220 race, and the 440-yard event in 51.4 seconds. The legends of Eric Liddell's sportsmanship were well known by then, and he was followed by an adoring throng wherever he went, scarcely able to move among the crowd.

The rules of athletics eligibility were not as strict as they are today, so Eric ran for Edinburgh University at St. Andrews on May 30. The wind was as fierce as the competition, but Eric again won his three events: the 100, the 220, and the 440, the 50.2 second quarter-mile being his best effort. He then stayed over and preached in church the next morning.

The following Saturday, the Queen's Park Harriers sponsored their annual invitational at Hampden Park, Glasgow. Eric entered the 440-yard handicap, and he had to give up a huge lead of ten yards. He repeated the previous week's 50.2 second performance, but could only pull up to third place. Before a crowd of over ten thousand fans, however, he anchored the Edinburgh mile-relay unit to a crushing thirty-yard victory. He also stayed overnight in Glasgow for Sunday speaking appearances.

The next Wednesday, June 10, Eric appeared in the Corstorphine "East of Scotland" Championship. He won the 440 and good-naturedly agreed to appear in a handicap 600-yard race. He asked for no qualifying heats, thinking to spare himself several extra races and not grasping that every runner in the district would turn out to race the champion. He was started fifteen yards back from the pack of 34 runners and never could split through the crowd, finishing seventh with a shy grin on his face.

But the East of Scotland Championships at Edinburgh's Powderhall track the following Saturday was serious racing. Eric won the 100-, the 220-, and the 300-yard races, overtaking several runners in the 220 from a handicap start and coming within three-tenths of a second of Wyndham Halswelle's 1908 native Scottish record at the 300-yard distance. The meet included a gymnastics demonstration by some high school boys who were thrilled when Eric spent time talking with them between events.

Eric's plan to enter the foreign missions meant that the spring 1925 would be his last racing season in Scotland. On Wednesday, June 24, he competed in Edinburgh for the last time in the Edinburgh Pharmacy Athletic Club 30th Annual Sports at Powderhall. He spotted an incredible eight yards in the 120-yard handicap and ran it in 12.0 seconds, finishing second by inches. He won sensationally in the mile-medley relay, a pair of 220-yard sprints, an 880-yard run, and a quarter-mile anchor leg. He started his anchor leg ten yards behind his opponent and won it by six. The press was becoming rhapsodic now, using headlines like "Scotland's Greatest Athlete" and "A Sight for the Gods."

That Saturday, June 27, 1925, Eric appeared in his final sports event in Scotland, the Scottish AAA Championship at Hampden Park, Glasgow. The Glasgow Students' Evangelical Union planned to turn the track meet into a series of mammoth religious rallies. For Eric, it was a sporting performance equal in merit to his Stamford Bridge performance in 1923 and his Olympic effort in 1924. The pressure on a reigning champion is tremendous in a big event. The newspapers ran column after column about the upcoming appearance of the man who held the sprint records, about the new runners who would challenge him, and how Eric would leave for China within a week of the meet.

Many were turned away from the stadium. The twelve thousand fans who got tickets witnessed superb performances from a number of fine young runners who later competed in the 1928 Olympics. Eric won the 100-yard sprint in 10.0, besting the runner-up by inches. He won the 220-yard race in 22.2 seconds, which was faster than his Olympic bronze medal effort in the 200 meters.

The crowd roared as Eric stormed to a first-place finish in the 440 with a personal best time of 49.2 seconds. This would convert to a 48.9 time for the 400-meter distance, which was even more remarkable on the slow Glasgow track. Eric's final race delighted the crowd: he overcame a five-yard deficit on his leg of the mile relay and won by ten yards.

It took a long time to quiet the crowd before Eric could be presented the Crabbie Cup, given to the top track and field athlete in Scotland each year. He tied for it in 1922 and won it outright in 1923, 1924, and 1925. No one else has since even come close to this performance, even though the proud little country has produced several Olympic champions.

Later, at a press interview, Eric stated, "I am glad to say that the prospects for athletics in Scotland are much better than when I made my first appearance on the track. Competition is keener, the achievements are better, and the amateur sport stands on a much higher pinnacle than it did. My best wishes go with those who will be chosen tonight to represent their country at the forthcoming contests against England and Ireland."

And at the awards ceremony for the Championship Cups, he was equally brief. "My motto in life has ever been, 'If a thing is worth doing, it is worth doing well.' I leave the track after four years."

The following day, Eric appeared in the Renfield Street United Free Church for his farewell to Glasgow. The crowd was so great that he had to go to another church and repeat his message. He told his enthralled audience how he had been afraid to speak in public in early 1923, and how he had written to Jenny about it. He related the message from her letter to him: "Fear not, for I am with thee; do not dismay, for I will guide thee."

Eric then went back to 29 Hope Terrace in Edinburgh to pack his bags. The Glasgow newspapers ran a poem that day:

> For China now another race he runs,
>> As sure and straight as those Olympic ones,
> And if the ending's not so simply known—
>> We'll judge he'll make it, since his speed's his own.

The departure services in Edinburgh were held before standing-room-only crowds at the YMCA and the St. Augustine Scottish Congregational Church. Eric had passed his divinity academics at the Congregational College and lacked only a special pre-ordination term, which he would take on his first furlough from China.

Eric's departure was quite an event. He readied himself to go by train to take the steamer packet, then take the Trans-Siberian Railroad all the way to China. Four big suitcases stood ready in the door of the mansion of 29 Hope Terrace, and a carriage drew up, pulled by the athletes from Edinburgh University. It was festooned with ribbons of white and blue, and behind it came dozens of women students. Eric got in, piled up his luggage, and waved to the neighbors. The procession traveled right up the main artery to Princess Street, starting as a parade, then becoming a religious rally. People marched by the hundreds to see him off.

The students made a miscalculation and entered the ramp that leads down to the Waverley Station platform from the wrong side. This made it impossible to board the train, and so they backed out and tried again.

After he boarded the train, hundreds ran alongside Eric's car grabbing his hand and calling for a speech. The engineer held up the train, and Eric, smiling from the train window tried to shout a few words. No one could hear him in the clamor, so he started singing "Jesus Shall Reign Where'er the Sun," and the crowd picked it up. The singing spread outward, down the platform, and up the ramp. People passing by on the street above even picked up the tune and joined in. It went on, verse after verse, as the train drew away.

In Eric's hand, for reading on the long trip, was a disturbing annual report from China written by his father. It told about political instability, fighting, and challenges to the missionary presence. Ahead of Eric was a very tough race. Behind him lay the greatest campaign of Christian witnessing through championship athletics that Scotland had ever seen.

Eric had been the Baron Coubertin's perfect Olympic model; Dr. Almond's holy alliance of Christianity with the athlete; the embodiment of the University of Pennsylvania's motto that became the philosophy of the Olympic Games and it was all due to the fact that he wanted to be a missionary in China like his father.

Photo Section

The Liddell family, with grandfather Robert Liddell in the center,
and grandchildren Jenny, Robbie, and Eric at his feet. Eric's parents are
second and third from the left in the back row.

Edinburgh Evangelistic Union

SPECIAL SERVICES

FOR YOUNG MEN AND WOMEN
(5th to 17th May)

Sundays   USHER HALL   .   . at 8.0
Week-days St. George's U.F. Church at 7.30

Convener
Mr. ERIC H. LIDDELL, B.Sc.

Leader
Mr. D. P. THOMSON, M.A.

NOTE.—*The Sunday Night Meetings in Usher Hall at 8 o'clock are open to everybody—old and young.*

B. S. O.

A printed announcement for Eric's first evangelistic speaking engagement, held in the spring of 1923 at Armadale, West Lothian.

The United Free Church, which was Presbyterian, where the family worshipped in Drymen.

Faith

A. A young man of 21. Pale face, tall lithe, serious.
   a. A solitary walk—on the edge of a precipice.
      Introspective—irritated—
      On the verge of the greatest discovery of his life.
     (Leader—pathfinder—pioneer.)
   b. Not long after—another solitary walk.
      Aminated, face lit up—the great discovery was made.
B. What was the discovery?
   1st walk. What shall I do?

Discovery

Not what I am—but what God is
Not what shall I do—but what God has done.
  Eyes on himself—Place them on God
  Eyes on his actions—Place them on God's
C. Have I nothing to do then?
    Yes, nothing but believe.
Rom. 10 "If thou shalt confess with thy mouth Jesus is Lord
& believe in thine heart that God hath raised him from
the dead, thou shalt be saved."

Notes for a sermon taken from Eric's Bible.

Scottish fans of Eric said he "culdna' lose when his heid's back."

Eric winning the furlong in 1923 at the English Amateur
Athletic Association Championships, where he also won the
100-yards in a record time of 9.7 seconds.

In the 1924 Paris Olympics, even though placed in the outside lane,
and choosing to run the race flat out from the gun, Eric won the 400-meters
with a world and Olympic record of 47.6 seconds.

BRITISH OLYMPIC CHAMPION
IN THE PULPIT

Instead of running in the Olympic Games, Eric Liddell (left), Olympic record breaker and Scottish Rugby International, preached at the Scottish Presbyterian Church in Paris on Sunday. If we had been

The Sunday following his win in the 400-meters, Eric preached in the Scots Kirk in Paris instead of participating in that day's Olympic events. Here he is shown with the minister of the congregation after the service.

A week after the 1924 Olympics, Eric graduated from Edinburgh University. Following the graduation ceremonies, Eric was 'chaired' from the Hall by fellow students, and crowned with a victor's laurel.

CHINA

Peking•
Tientsin•
Siaochang•

YELLOW
SEA

Located between Siaochang and Peking, Tientsin felt the pressures of the escalating war between Japan and China.

After returning to Tientsin, China in 1925 to being teaching at The Anglo-Chinese College (TACC), Eric found additional opportunities for Christian work, such as teaching this Bible class at Union Church. Eric is on the far right.

Taken in 1929 at Pei-Tai-Ho, this was one of the final
family 'sittings' before James and Mary Liddell returned to Britain.
Also pictured are Rob's wife, Ria, and baby daughter.

In 1934, at Tientsin, Eric married Florence Mackenzie,
the daughter of a Canadian missionary.

Eric and Florence in Scotland in 1940 with two older daughters.

...is rather in the day). When my cart was about 20 miles from our hospital (carrying one wounded man) I heard that there was another man a mile away who I might pick up by going very slightly out of the way. When we reached the village I was led to an outhouse & there I found a man who had been wounded four or five days before. He had been one of six who were executed but seeing he wouldn't bend down like the others and the officer drew his sword & slashed at him. He fell as dead & the troops moved on. The villagers coming out later found him still alive and put him in the outhouse where they tended him. He decided to come with me, sitting on the shafts of the cart. For next ten miles we were travelling almost parallel with the Japanese forces but gradually they went further South.

At Hospital he not only recovered but became a Christian and in gratitude painted several pictures for me to take away & sell for the Hospital Girls' work. I chose this picture - the Peony, the flower of China, as being both beautiful & I liked the saying on it "she is the most beautiful in the city (China), her modesty & manner come from god". The name of the painter is Li Han Shang

he has written the two words 'Li Sheng Han Shang' under his seal.

May I/A We all you hope it will be, bringing joy, peace & quiet happiness to you & your husband (I'm sorry I don't know his name).

Yours very sincerely,
Eric M Liddell

Dear Elsa,

First of all let me send my very heartiest congratulations on your marriage, I only wish I could have been at it to give the congratulations in person. I heard that you were in Hong Kong and it was only a week or two ago that I heard that you hadn't actually left but that the war had changed your plans. May you have the happiness you well deserve and many years of it.

Thank you for the Christmas card with its greetings. I expect you have heard that we decided it would be best for Florence and the two children to stay in Toronto and for me to come over alone. The Society are however keeping me busy till May when I hope to return to join the family for a few months holiday before going on to China.

It's wonderful to be back. The dampness in the air is very refreshing after the dryness of China.

I'm enclosing a lithographed picture which I thought you might like. Actually the story associated with it is rather interesting. When my cart was about 20 miles from our hospital (carrying one wounded man) I heard that there was another man a mile away who I might pick up by going very slightly out of the way. When we reached the village I was led to an outhouse and there I found a man who had been wounded four or five days before. He had been one of six who were executed but actually he wouldn't bend down like the others and the officer drew his sword and slashed at him. He fell as dead & all the troops moved on. The villagers coming out later found him still alive and put him in the outhouse where they tended him. He decided to come with me, sitting on the shafts of the cart. For about ten miles we were travelling about parallel with the Japanese forces, but gradually they went further south.

At Hospital he not only recovered but became a Christian and in gratitude painted several pictures for me to take away and sell for the Hospital & its work. I chose this picture—the Peony, the flower of China, as being both beautiful and I like the saying on it, "She is the most beautiful in the city (China), her modesty and manner come from God." The name of the painter is Li Hsin Sheng. He has written the two words '心 生 Hsin Sheng above his seal.

May 1940 be all you hope it will be bringing joy and peace & full happiness to you and your husband.

Yours very sincerely,
Eric H. Liddell

A portrait of Eric Liddell taken shortly before his death in 1945.

"Know ye not that they which run in a race run all, but one receiveth the prize? So run, that ye may obtain. And every man that striveth for the mastery is temperate in all things. Now they do it to obtain a corruptible crown; but we an incorruptible."
1 Corinthians 9:24, 25

Part II

The Missionary

*E**ric Liddell's association* with the East coincided with political turmoil and explosive reaction against foreign influence. He had been born in China in the wake of the Boxer Rebellion, which created a climate that was inauspicious for European and American missionaries, and he returned when there there was a violent uprising against Europeans.

The calling to which Eric responded must be understood in terms of the life of the remarkable men and women of the China missionary movement in the last century of the Manchu dynasty. Eric was raised to be one of the band of gentle Christian knights who spent their lives heroically spreading the gospel through the missions. He was truly at home with these people—they had reared and educated him, and deeply influenced the direction of his life.

The broad sweep of historical events leading to the political climate to which Eric returned is too large and complex to present in depth here. Certain events did, however, impact upon Eric's life directly. It is important to see these in their historical context in order to understand better the twentieth-century missionary presence in China.

Western missionary influence in China began with Marco Polo's "discovery" in the late thirteenth century. A very profitable trade route was soon opened, which provided the opportunity for the Society of Jesus (the Jesuits) to begin work there among the people. They were scholarly, aggressive, and dedicated men. Father Matteo Ricci, the first to penetrate the closed Chinese society, arrived in 1583. By 1601 he had set up a permanent mission, learning to handle with admirable skill problems like the resentment of Chinese scholars at his Italian map, which showed Europe at the center of the world and China in distorted form at the margin. The Jesuit priest simply redrew the map with China at the center. This was the kind of sensitivity and respect Eric Liddell also demonstrated during his missionary years.

Though the Jesuit effort began with great promise, over the next few centuries European influence in the Far East was focused more on trade than religion. The seventeenth-century European wars that followed the Reformation substantially weakened the missions in China. During the eighteenth century, as Western nations vied with one another for economic advantages, some traders employed strong measures to coerce individual Chinese seaports to agree to terms favorable to the Europeans. The Manchus had only recently taken over the Chinese government, having overthrown the ancient M'ing Dynasty, and were too weak militarily to oppose such practices.

Following the American War of Independence, British foreign policy shifted its emphasis towards the Far East. They soon confronted a difficult issue regarding the common trading currency. Opium, which was mostly grown in India, had long served as the medium of exchange in the Orient. Members of Parliament raised a strong moral objection, but government officials countered that the local merchants insisted on this form of currency, which forced the British to conform to this age-old practice.

A large majority of Western traders did use opium as currency. A letter published by the widow of the Reverend Robert Morrison, a long-time U.S. missionary at Canton (Guangzhou), reported that Mr. D.W.C. Olyphant was the only American merchant at that great seaport who did not deal in opium. She characterized him as "a pious, devoted servant of Christ, and a friend of China."

Britain's and France's interests became so tied up with the opium trade that they went to war with China in 1839 when Governor Lin Tse-hsu of the Hunan and Hopei Provinces seized the opium factories in his district. He ordered his officials to stop trading in the drug, which had brought so much suffering to his people, and sent a letter of protest to Queen Victoria.

Great Britain and France mobilized their military and naval forces and soon re-captured the giant seaport opium factories. The so-called "Opium War" was settled by the Peace of Nanking in 1842, which was negotiated by Lord Palmerston, one of the British Foreign Ministers who put teeth in the *pax britannica*. China was required to pay an indemnity and dedicate certain ports and facilities to the European powers who therefore could control the trading terms in the three-way exchange of opium, silver, and Chinese export commodities.

Westerners in China were often endangered by the wars and internal rebellions of the nineteenth century. In 1850 a great social and political upheaval began in the central coastal provinces. The Taiping Rebellion, as it was known, raged for fifteen years before the Manchu government was able to defeat it. Many European and American missionaries lost their lives during the uprising, partly because they were often specifically targeted by groups accusing them of being the catalysts behind the revolt.

Meanwhile, a tremendous wave of evangelism had swept Britain and American at the dawn of the nineteenth century. An important element in this movement was the London Missionary Society, which had established a functional presence in China by 1807. To some of the idealistic missionaries, it was a chance to serve God by making converts for Christ in an ancient culture. For others, it was a career in Christian atonement for the evil inflicted upon the Chinese by the opium trade.

The work of missionaries was particularly difficult and dangerous. Many of their efforts to effect social reform in China were turned against them. For example, some opposed the practice of binding the feet of young girls, which entailed forcing the child's big toe inward at a right angle and bending the other toes and the forward arch underneath with tightly wrapped strip bandages. This usually began at the age of five for girls of the privileged classes, causing them agonizing pain for several years and debilitated movement for the rest of their lives. The priests and the Mandarin scholars defended the practice vigorously, however, and accused the missionaries who opposed it of turning wives against their husbands and daughters against families.

Those who profited from the opium traffic made missionary opposition to it appear as a sign of Western interference in Chinese internal affairs. Advances in medicine were twisted by Chinese physicians to seem immoral, hypocritical, or deceitful. Some openly questioned why the God of the Westerners, who supposedly practiced such a superior form of saving men, was unable to save His own life. Such arguments were powerfully effective in a society of such ancient oral tradition, one in which 80 percent of the people could not read. It succeeded in whipping up vehement anti-missionary sentiment.

That decade also saw two other significant military events in the Orient. United States Navy Commodore Matthew C. Perry brought a powerful fleet to Japan in 1853, and obtained a trade treaty that left the Japanese political leadership intact and established America as a new maritime power in the region.

Five years later, in China, the skipper of the trading junk *Lorcha* baited the Royal Navy by insulting the Union Jack. The *"Lorcha* affair" mushroomed into the two-year conflict known as the Arrow War, or the second Opium War. British and French troops were sent to China with powerful fleet cannons in support, and punitive actions were ordered by Lord Palmerston, who was then Prime Minister. Queen Victoria lost confidence in Palmerston over the affair, believing that he had acted without her knowledge in a way that left her powerless to order the campaign stopped. The punitive expeditions sailed thirty miles up the Haiho River to Tientsin and then marched overland to Peking. They quickly seized the Manchu capital, clearly demonstrating the real weakness of the Imperial government. Some soliders sacked the Summer Palace and the Forbidden City, both of which held holy, mystical qualities for the Chinese.

Even though the British government instituted a policy of economic development in northern China shortly thereafter that led to the construction of railroads and factories, the bitterness among Chinese, though not uniform, remained.

In 1870, local religious and administrative authorities stirred up a violent attack against the Westerners, particularly the missionaries at Tientsin. The French compound for families of the non-Chinese community, which was surrounded by a wall and had guards at the gate, was severely attacked because it was seen as a symbolic affront to Chinese autonomy. Entire missionary families were martyred there. Heavy casualties also were inflicted by the Anglo-French punitive force that came to rescue the westerners and to restore order. Thus, the century preceding Eric's missionary service was colored by two patterns in China: the missionaries as a disruptive branch of Western colonialism, and the missionaries as heroic messengers of Christ.

Meanwhile, Britain in the mid-nineteenth century was undergoing developments that would be significant in Eric Liddell's life, particularly the development of the British boarding school system. The London Missionary Society, the organization in which Eric and his family served, created organized a boarding school at Walthamstow in 1841 for the sons of its overseas missionaries. This society was part of the wave of evangelism that swept Britain and America early in the nineteenth century. The school evolved into Eltham College, Eric Liddell's training ground for becoming a hero of the foreign missionary service.

The traditions and teachings of the British boarding school system were determinative factors in molding Eric's talents to fit the mission to which he was called. Dr. Thomas Arnold, the vigorous young headmaster at Rugby Preparatory School, was largely responsible for the system's growth and development. It was often described as *the* system for training the future managers of the British Empire.

The concept of the schools was based upon two educational principles. First, a student's development must address three dimensions of the person: scholastic or intellectual, moral, and physical. Second, the schools offered a community environment in which to teach such lessons, with one faculty member specifically designated to tutor the boys of each form, or grade level, for several years.

The idea of a school for the sons of the missionaries serving in China was precipitated by family and career needs, but from its early days the school sought and applied the soundest of the boarding school principles. These included loving discipline, training in good citizenship, leadership through team sports, and instilling Christian foundations and observances in the young men.

Dr. Arnold died in 1842 at the age of forty-seven, but his work was carried on through his children, colleagues, and graduates. His network of ideas soon influenced existing schools at Sherbourne, Haileybury, Repton, Uppington, Felts, and Winchester. The Rugby Movement, as it was called, then spread to newer schools such as Cheltenham, Marlborough, Wellington, Rossall, and Clifton. (Dr. Arnold later became legendary through Thomas Hughes' 1857 novel *Tom Brown's School Days,* which was the basis for a popular mini-series in the early 1970s.)

The principles behind the British educational system were the basis of a plan proposed by the Reverend James Hudson Taylor in 1872 to the London Council of the China Inland Mission Society. He emphatically exclaimed, "Why do we not send our missionaries to China? That is the country to aim at, with its teeming population, its strong, intelligent, scholarly people!" He proposed that the Society, which was a functional partner of the London Missionary Society, bring the gospel to the rural people of northern China through adapting the principles and practices of British education.

They agreed and decided to do something a bit different in the northeast China mission: they would send men with the same strong, gentlemanly personality that was characteristic of pastors of the British overseas missionary service, but the men chosen for this service would be missionary *athletes,* recruited primarily from Oxford, Cambridge and Edinburgh Universities. The Council also hoped that its own college would eventually produce men strong enough for such a test. The idea of teaching athletics to Chinese boys, whose culture opposed it, was an afterthought.

The China Inland Mission took its appeal beyond the prep schools to the peak of the British university system. The first large-scale recruitment of student volunteers for missionary service was in 1884 in a series of meetings at Oxford and Cambridge. Dozens answered the call, including a group of highly successful athletes from Cambridge who soon discovered that they had an unusual ability to persuade students to support Christian principles and to volunteer for the missionary service. These athletes became known as the "Cambridge Seven."

There was something about these muscular young scholar-athletes that the clever agnostics and the doubters could not gainsay. The impact on young students, already awed by the expansion of their intellectual horizons in college and floundering for commitment, was simply tremendous. When the "Cambridge Seven" took the train to Edinburgh University for a religious witnessing and recruitment campaign, a local professor wrote:

> Many had heard of Stanley Smith [a rugby star], and to everyone who knew anything of cricket the name Studd is familiar. And so the word went round our classrooms, "Let us go and give the athlete missionaries a welcome!" The men gathered—about 1,000 . . . The students were spellbound. The two speakers were so manly—types indeed of handsome, healthy manhood—were so happy . . . when they had done, hundreds of student crowded round them to grasp their hand, followed them to the train by which they were going right off to London, and were on the platform saying "God speed you."

The movement of athletes in religious service had some powerful roots in America, too. President Ulysses S. Grant had received his version in the 1870s of Queen Victoria's 1839 protest from China about the opium trade. It was a polite rational complaint against the practice of importing unemployed Chinese citizens through contract recruiting companies to use them for cheap labor. For instance, they were "employed" to build the Panama Railroad and the U.S. Transcontinental Railroad, but they were consigned to a life of social and economic prejudice in segregated communities. There were American missionaries abroad who wrote to their home boards asking that U.S. citizens become aware of the moral tensions implicit in foreign missionary work.

The American Bible Society had long been using business and technological know-how to export millions of Bibles and religious tracts into dozens of languages around the world. Dwight L. Moody, the Massachusetts shoe salesmen-turned-evangelist, was spellbinding audiences with his passionate Christian speaking and organizing missionary training schools. He made fact-finding tours of the British educational and religious training system in the 1870s and returned for another series of tours in the 1880s, when the Baron Coubertin was doing similar work. Sharing the pulpit with Scottish evangelist Henry Drummond, his preaching sparked a movement that brought James Liddell to the ministry.

Ira David Sankey, an American hymn writer, joined Moody on his tour of British schooling and evangelical efforts. Sankey's unforgettable lyrics and tunes were published in 1875 as *Gospel Hymns,* a series that was continued and revised in a highly popular 1891 edition. They were to become Eric Liddell's favorites, for he had grown up with them, and he would personally translate and teach them to his Chinese students a half century later. In addition, college students at Harvard, Yale, and Princeton conducted evangelical campaigns just as their counterparts were doing at Oxford and Cambridge.

The London Missionary Society (LMS), concentrated its twentieth century work at the "treaty ports" in China, setting up Christian colleges for the sons of the managerial class. The China Inland Mission (CIM) focused its efforts upon the rural zones. While James Gilmour of the CIM was the force that brought Eric's father to China, James Liddell transfered to the LMS during Eric's boyhood. Eric's career would be in reverse of his father's—first at an LMS college, and then a rural, missionary beat.

The early twentieth century was a critical time for Christian evangelists in China. Industrial development had brought social change to the people of the north China plain. Thousands of village laborers saw their jobs and their values at risk before the onslaught of railroads, steam tugs, mechanical digging machines, telegraph systems, and other fruits of Western technological civilization. And in time, Eric and Rob Liddell would be shining examples of those scholar-athletes who gave their lives to the Lord's service in a country experiencing turmoil on all horizons.

*A*s *Eric's train clattered* across Europe and Asia on the Trans-Siberian Railway, Eric had ample time to consider his father's report to the London Missionary Society, written in December 1924. The Reverend James Liddell spoke of political turbulence, rebellion, civil war, floods, and famine. "Oh, the horror of it all!" stated this godly man who loved the Chinese people. "And to think that so much of it is needless suffering, destruction and waste. . . . It is not surprising that during part of this year church work has been so difficult."

Yet as recently as April 1922 it had all seemed propitious. The World Student Christian Federation Conference had taken place that month in Peking. The following October some twelve hundred delegates, half of them Chinese, met at Shanghai where a giant compendium of Christian evangelical work was compiled.

But the picture was mixed. Officially, the Kuomintang Party advocated educational advancement and sent thousands of students abroad to study. There was support for Western colleges within China; indeed, Peking had become the most important center of higher education in that part of the world. The Peking Union Medical College had strong leadership from the Western medical missionaries and was later credited even by post-Revolutionary Chinese leaders as a founding cornerstone of the Chinese medical system. Yet there was also intellectual ferment at Peking, some of it rooted in ancient antagonisms between the Manchus and the earlier dynasties.

In 1924, the Kuomintang's first Party Convention at Canton had enunciated the high-toned, democratic principles of Dr. Sun Yat-sen. The following year, however, he died. The old scourge of regional warlordism resurfaced, and it was complicated by the presence of the several foreign treaty ports, the pressures from Japan for a sphere of influence in Manchuria, and the new Chinese Communist Party. This group, of course, held out promise for the Soviet Union to gain a foothold in China, too. The simultaneous existence of several forces that seemed mutually exclusive was not a new set of circumstances.

On May 30, 1925, there was an incident in Shanghai between student demonstrators, who were angry at the foreign political autonomy in a major Chinese city, and municipal authorities. British police fired their guns in what they felt was legitimate self-protection, and a wave of rioting and anti-Western protest ensued. This led to a struggle within the Kuomintang which would eventually propel Chiang Kai-shek into power, with his officer clique from the Whampoa Military Academy as the political binding force. This was the confused milieu in which Eric Liddell found the land of his birth upon his return.

The Trans-Siberian Railway cuts southest across China to Peking, then turns to the coast of the Po Hai (Gulf of Chihli) where, 170 miles up the coast from Taku, the several missionary services maintained their seaside retreat. On July 18, Eric was met at the train station in Pei-tei-ho. His parents, Jenny, and Ernest were there to meet him. They had not seen each other since the departure at Waverley Station in Edinburgh in October 1922. While Eric's admirers in Edinburgh had sent a telegram, followed by newspaper clippings about the tumultuous last days in Edinburgh, there still was much to share. And Eric's delivery of London Missionary Society documents just over two weeks from their dispatch in Britain represented about the best courier service that the world had at the time.

A week after Eric arrived, Rob and his wife arrived on the coastal packet from Shanghai. For five weeks they stayed at the big brick bungalow with a wide veranda overlooking the gulf. Another missionary from Scotland, Miss Annie Buchan, arrived for a holiday with some of her Mandarin Chinese language school classmates from Peking. The school, funded by the Rockefeller Foundation, had students from the business, government, and missionary communities of several western countries. Miss Annie related some of the student and political unrest in Peking, while Rob told of similar problems down at Shanghai. And yet the scene was idyllic at Pei-tei-ho.

In September, Miss Buchan was assigned to the town that was Eric's first home in China, Siaochang. This mission station was thriving, as was the sister station at Tsangchow, but the populous Hopei plain was seething amid a horrible civil war. So Miss Annie was off, first by rail and then by mule cart, to a rugged assignment; and Eric headed for Tientsin, where the environment seemed charming to the casual observer.

Tientsin, today an industrial metropolis, was already a booming city in 1925, second largest in the northeast behind Peking. The ancient Chinese heart of the city had a few elegant neighborhoods, but there were huge, teeming districts that seemed overwhelming to the Western eye. The foreign enclaves, minus the ones recently wrested from the losers of World War I, were visibly better in their standard of living than that afforded to the average native. This was a morally difficult situation for Western missionaries who had come to teach and convert. In discussions about communism and democracy, twentieth-century revolutionary romantics have often tended to exaggerate in saying that the middle or professional class is non-existent in developing nations, but the fact is that Tientsin had a substantial middle class in 1925. And these were the Chinese with whom Eric was to have most of his contact for the next twelve years.

The Western community was still anchored by a significant military force from Britain, France, and the United States. At one time thirty thousand Western troops had been there in 1901 to recapture the legations and protect Westerners during the Boxer Rebellion. By 1925, this number was one third as high, although there was back-up available from the fleets in the China Sea.

The missionary community in Tientsin contained a wide variety of Catholic and Protestant faiths. There were three offices of the world's great Bible societies: British and Foreign, Scottish National, and American. The American YMCA had a unit that dated back to 1895. The London Missionary Society, though not the largest, was highly respected, and its Mackenzie Memorial Hospital was vital to the area. The China Inland Mission Society, whose mission stations were in the outer regions, had a headquarters station at Tientsin.

The London Missionary Society had its facilities within the French, rather than the British, concession. The Tientsin Anglo-Chinese College (TACC) was one of three intermediate level schools operated by foreign missionaries. The American Methodist School and the French Roman Catholic School also taught young Chinese boys and men in the age group of twelve to twenty. Dr. Lavington Hart, the founder of the Tientsin Anglo-Chinese College, was still its active principal. The school had twenty-five Chinese teachers and five British faculty, one of whom was Professor A.P. Cullen, Eric's long-time science teacher at Eltham College.

The five hundred Chinese students came from middle class and professional families, the majority of them from non-Christian families. Since the school's earliest years, there had been both day students and boarders. The boys walked into the French enclave about 7:30 each morning, dressed in their long blue robes. The robe was a symbol of status; taking it off for the rough-and-tumble of athletics was seen as a crude western custom.

Ideologically, the students were under family and governmental pressure to modernize, to acquire the skills of the Westerner, but not all of them received strong encouragement to become Christians. This issue was handled gently at the TAC College, where Bible classes were voluntary. Nevertheless, the forty to fifty graduates who passed out of the school each year went on to fine Chinese or foreign universities and, while no one has written a systematic study of their influence over the Communist Revolution, they were certainly part of the transitional modernizing forces in China. Collectively, the three intermediate foreign-operated schools at Tientsin had a significant impact on northeast China.

While Eric was thus employed, his family also had diversified duties. The Reverend J.D. Liddell maintained a pastorate in Tientsin and several visiting pastorates in the interior, and he worked with a network of Chinese pastors to encourage leadership development. Mrs. Mary Liddell maintained the family home as a kind of missionary activity center with luncheons, dinners, Bible campaigns, meetings, and a vigorous program of outreach visitation. Rob, of course, was on the medical staff at Shanghai. Jenny taught the kindergarten at the British Grammar School and played the piano for a wide variety of school and church occasions.

Eric taught at the TACC and at the Sunday school. He also was the athletics department head at the TACC, and the unofficial kingpin in area sporting events among both Westerners and Chinese.

Ernest attended the grammar school and, for the first time, came under the regular influence of his famous older brother.

Eric was made the science teacher at the college as his primary assignment. Even though the classes all were conducted in English, some of the Chinese boys had only a rote knowledge of the foreign language. Since English was deemed necessary by the Chinese government for the process of acquiring the fruits of Western civilization, the boys were under pressure to learn it. But Eric had no training at all in that kind of teaching, and ultimately, helping the boys learn English helped him develop a mastery of Mandarin Chinese.

South at Siaochang the call came for medical volunteers in December 1925. The anti-western forces of warlord Li Ching Lin were locked in terrible struggle against the troops of the so called "Christian" general, Feng Yu Hsiang. Miss Annie Buchan joined up with volunteers assembling at the sister mission in Tsangchow, and from there they went to Nan Yuan, near the outskirts of Peking. A volunteer staff brought equipment out from the Peking Union Medical College to tend the pitiful rows of wounded and dying soldiers. General Feng visited his wounded troops in the temporary shelters, and the staff never knew when the war might erupt right there because wounded men from both armies were brought in for care.

Christmas found Tientsin embroiled in the struggle since Feng's troops had laid siege on December 3. While General Li Ching Lin was anti-Western, he did not dare threaten the western community; they were protected by treaty and by their own military and naval forces. But the war resulted in high casualties among Chinese in the district, and Chinese Christians were greatly relieved when General Feng's troops stormed the city and took control of all but the treaty enclaves on Christmas Eve. Unfortunately, Feng's forces had been defeated heavily in the interior on December 18, so the missionaries lived amid political uncertainty that first Christmas Eric was in China.

The following month the war went in favor of the pro-Christian forces, and the Kuomintang government seemed to be gaining power.

In January 1926 Eric mounted all his newspaper cuttings into big albums. A Chinese carpenter made a lovely pair of wooden cases with lids for his collection of nearly two hundred track and rugby medals. The Olympic gold medal, of course, was the one thing that everyone wanted to see; but from the very beginning, Eric avoided any conversation about his Olympic stardom. Nevertheless, he and Jenny had an active social life among the Westerners in Tientsin. He was a coveted guest in the drawing room and at the dinner table; yet people always expressed surprise that he seemed more interested in their own achievements than in talking about his. That same month, Eric was invited to be the speaker at the Union Church Literary and Social Guild, and it was strongly hinted that people would like to hear about the Olympic Games. He decided to put the matter on record, since he was asked about it so often.

"If I take a fish," he told the packed audience, "enjoying all the freedom it does in the sea, and ruthlessly cast it onto the heated sand, then ask it to breathe, I am asking it to do the impossible. I am asking it to break the law of environment; it cannot breathe, it only gasps. Similarly, if you take an athlete away from his proper sphere, his thin clothing and his fresh air, give him a stiff shirt and a collar that catches his neck each time he tries to turn, then on top of all that ask him to speak, you are asking him to break what I call the law of environment. He cannot speak; he can only gasp!

"When the spirits have been drooping and the material is slow in coming forward, one thing has ever kept my head above water, and that is, I am a Scot. It seems rather a strange kind of reason to give, yet when we go beneath the surface to the second part of the reason, we find where the truth lies. If one gives a paper to this Guild, one becomes a member free of charge; if not, the fee is two (Chinese) dollars. Hence, even in my times of greatest depression, I have still struggled on."

This droll bit of Scottish spoofing about tightfistedness set the audience laughing wildly. Sir Harry Lauder told funnier Scottish jokes, but Eric, after all, was an Olympic hero who always told something funny and self-effacing. And then, Eric rapidly named the major track meets that had led to Paris, and the way in which he viewed the entire process as part of the committed life.

That spring, Eric organized the Annual College Sport in April. He ran an exhibition race and succeeded in increasing participation among the Chinese boys, which was the purpose for the race. In the summer, before the family went to the beach at Pei-tai-ho, Eric was introduced by his parents to Mr. and Mrs. Hugh Mackenzie, who had just returned from furlough.

When Reverend and Mrs. Liddell had moved to Tientsin from Peking they had initially lived at #2 Taku Road, and had moved to #6 on the same street when Eric arrived. The Mackenzies lived a short distance away at #70 Cambridge Road. They were Canadian missionaries who worked at the hospital that bore their family name, but were not related to its founder. The meeting took place in the vestibule of the Union Church at mid-week Prayer Meeting. This was the church the missionary families attended, apart from the church where they held services for the Chinese converts, which was on the compound. The Mackenzies were immediately impressed with Eric's modesty. Eric was hardly aware at the time that he was meeting his future in-laws.

That summer, down at Siaochang where they had seen such terrible political conflict, there was a flash flood that carried away the hospital and several of the buildings. Resources were insufficient to provide a staff doctor, and rebuilding had to be postponed too.

The following spring, the combination of structural damage and danger from the warlord armies was so great a problem that the British Consul at Tientsin ordered the evacuation of the L.M.S. mission at Siaochang. For five months Miss Annie Buchan and the medical mission staff worked out of the Mackenzie Hospital at Tientsin. In August of 1926 Eric's family enjoyed their summer retreat to Pei-tei-ho, but they were very concerned for their future.

Things looked better in the next year for the future of a Western Christian presence in China. Chang Kai-shek's forces had won a big victory, securing a political seat at Hankow. And he set up a permanent seat of government at Nanking that would endure until 1936. He formally broke with the Communist Party in 1927, which was strong both at certain intellectual centers and in the interior of the north-western provinces. The Communists, while not as outwardly bigoted as the Boxers in anti-Western sentiment, were opposed to the missionary presence on the grounds that it was merely an arm of colonialism, a system by which to obtain Chinese subjugation to Western nations without soldiers. On June 4, 1928, Chiang Kai-shek captured Peking, consolidating the power of the Kuomintang government over the historic capital city.

In the spring of 1928, Eric had made good progress with his science teaching, and there seemed to be more acceptance of athletics among the Chinese. There was an increasing interest in sports because of the impending IXth Modern Olympiad scheduled for Amsterdam. Eric was not formally invited by the British AAA to participate, having communicated clearly and publicly to them in 1925 that he was now a missionary in China. Although some have claimed otherwise, there never was any controversy between Eric and the London Missionary Society staff about allowing him to compete. He did not ask to go; but had he made such a request, it would have been granted, and at no expense to the LMS. But there were stern demands upon the missonaries, especially at that time, and Eric felt that he was needed in China.

In May 1928, the restored Siaochang station once again had to evacuate to Tsangchow; the warlord armies were operating in a manner more accurately described as banditry. Miss Annie Buchan and the staff quickly boarded mule carts and started out on the treacherous journey. They found a Methodist Mission en route and took temporary refuge there. Soldiers were robbing the Chinese but let the missionaries enter the mission.

"We had been told," reported Miss Annie, "of how soldiers plundered the poor village people, and now we were seeing them at work kicking open doors, pushing their swords through them, hearing the cries of the terrified people inside. There was, of course, nothing to plunder from us, but once again we felt ashamed to go free. The band of soldiers were also ashamed for us to see what their fellow soldiers were doing and offered to escort us. We did not want that, however, knowing that we would be safer on our own.

"Very soon another band of soldiers caught up with us. They blamed us for having a bodyguard and for breaking treaty rights. Finally, they all came along with us, making us walk while they took turns riding upon the cart. Things were looking ugly. We were willing to walk but were not happy about the uneasy pace. Fortunately, for us, the enemy was on their tail and they ran off in front as fast as they could."

Conditions for the missionaries were dire. They had no real supplies, and they were caring for many victims of the war. But one general felt sorry for them; he assured the missionaries that he had no use for religion, but he sent over some food. A short while later his forces were defeated, and he was murdered about one mile from Siaochang.

The London Missionary Society had a way of sending in the first team when it was needed. In the fall of 1928, Dr. Rob Liddell arrived, along with his wife and daughter Peggie, to supervise the rebuilding of the Siaochang Mission Hospital and to become the Medical Superintendent there. He and his family were desperately sick in their early days at Siaochang, but they got the mission re-established, and the working relationship between "Dr. Rob" and Miss Annie would last well into World War II. Miss Annie, who now resides in Peterhead, Scotland, still likes to tell how Dr. Rob never started an operation without first saying a prayer.

At the end of 1928, Chiang Kai-shek consolidated control in the north, and Miss Annie recorded the missionary viewpoint of this event. She wrote, ". . . He was eager to see us advance in all aspects of our hospital work. Education was to have a higher standard; and . . . we saw the dawn of a new hope."

Meanwhile, the Emperor Hirohito in 1926 had ascended the imperial throne of Japan and, consistent with the saber-rattling policy of the military clique in his court, wanted to make an impression upon the rest of Asia. What better than a Far Eastern Games calculated to take place just after the Olympic Games at Port Arthur? This splendid seaport, which lies on the Liaoning Peninsula in Northeast China (formerly Lu-shun) anchors the northern entrance to the Po Hai. It was the military key to Japan's plan to take over Manchuria, and perhaps, one day, even Peking. So a huge stadium was constructed, and even if the running track was not quite up to Olympic standards, Eric Liddell was.

In the Olympics at Amsterdam, America's Ray Barbuti won the 400-meter race in a time that was slower than Eric's win at Paris in 1924. The best runner, Emerson Spencer, had set a new world record for the event in May but had been eliminated from his own event at the U.S. Olympic tryouts through an incredible coaching gaffe. So Eric's time at Paris still stood as the Olympic record; Douglas Lowe had repeated as 800-meter winner for the British team because the expected showdown with Germany's Dr. Otto Peltzer vanished when Peltzer became ill at the Games.

The French and Japanese track and field units came to the well-publicized Far Eastern Games at Port Arthur in October 1928. But it was Eric who won the 200-meter race in 21.8 seconds, which tied the winning time at Amsterdam by Canada's Percy Williams. The 400-meter race, in which the crowd of over fifty thousand people had great interest because of Eric's fame, Eric won easily in 47.8 seconds, tying Ray Barbuti's time at Amsterdam. Eric had thus tied two Olympic gold medal times running on a slow track against weak competition, with only a few serious training sessions in four years! Small wonder that track experts wrote how Eric was still the reigning quarter-miler.

When the 400-meter event ended at Port Arthur, Eric had a taxi standing by to rush him down to the dock, where the steamer for Tientsin was scheduled to leave fifteen minutes after the start of his final race. He first had to stand to attention for the playing of "God Save the King!" The band fell silent, and Eric prepared to race for his taxi. But the band had to play "Le Marseillaise" for the French runner who took the silver medal! With his coat pulled over his running outfit, bag in hand, Eric ran to the taxi, and the driver gave it his own racing best. As the taxi screeched to a stop on the wharf, the steamer was pulling away from the dock.

Eric ran to the edge and watched. A big tidal surge seemed to heave the steamer towards the pier, so Eric pitched his bag across to the deck. He backed up a dozen steps and did a running long jump of fifteen feet, over open water, from the dock to the pitching steamer deck. And he made it back to Tientsin for church services and Sunday school duties the next day. Comic books for young readers and sports pages in Scotland suddenly appeared with the "Flying Scot" sailing over new horizons—Olympic records, Asian political adventures, and rails of moving ships.

Eric's brother Rob had not been living in Scotland at the time of Eric's greatest athletic triumphs. A local track meet was set up so the residents of Tientsin could see their Olympic star in action. Fortunately, one practical improvement to the Siaochang Mission was its purchase of a motorcycle. Dr. Rob and Miss Annie made the maiden journey on the vehicle northward to Tientsin to watch the race. This mode of travel was, after all, no more undignified than pitching along on a mule cart.

At the track, the *Tientsin and Peking Times* photographer had a heavy new press camera with wooden tripod legs, just like his Western counterparts. But there had been little interest in competitive running in China, and consequently little awareness of how fast a sprinter could really go. The photographer moved out onto the track as the gun cracked, set up his equipment, and went under his cloth hood. He lined up his shot, fiddled with his lens, and adjusted the legs. He planned to focus on Mr. Liddell as the great runner approached the camera, get a highly unique photograph and . . . *CRASH!* Eric and the photographer were both knocked unconscious. Rob and Annie ran down onto the field and carried Eric into a tent.

When he came to, Eric merely smiled and said, "I was just winded."

Eric was not "winded" when he played several rugby matches with local civilian units against the British, French, and U.S. military detachments. The Western military garrisons had a friendly sports rivalry going in track, soccer, polo, tennis, and rugby. Soldiers gave some colorful reports on how they could not catch Eric at all, how he seemed to be a phantom on the field. It was to Eric's credit that his teams were often the victors, and in individual competition he regularly beat the regimental champions.

While Germany had lost their enclave in China through the Treaty of Versailles after World War I, there still were Germans working in China. Dr. Otto Peltzer, the reigning world record holder in the 500-meter event, the 880-yard distance, and the 1,500 meters came to China for a visit in the fall of 1929. It was suggested that Otto and Eric compete while Otto was in China. In their 400-meter special race, Eric won it in 49.1; there could be no doubt that, with any kind of serious training, he would have continued to break world records.

Peltzer, who already was in his thirties, beat Eric in the 800-meter race between them, and then encouraged Eric to enter that event in the 1932 Xth Olympiad, which already had been announced for Los Angeles. Eric thought he was too old, and Peltzer laughed, saying he would represent Germany at Los Angeles. Peltzer did enter the 800-meters in those Games, but he did not qualify for the finals.

He and Eric both expressed the prevailing European view that if the Games were held in the United States, most European athletes would not be able to compete because European nations did not subsidize training and travel expenses, publicly or privately, to the extent done in America. Subsequent national composition of the 1932 Games did reveal some reduction of competitors from outside the Western hemisphere, but not to the degree that Eric and Otto both feared in 1929. And Europeans who took this position generally overlooked the fact that the Games were intended to be worldwide, not European.

At the end of 1928, changes were in the wind for the missionaries. The generation that included Eric's parents and Dr. Lavington Hart at the TACC had been through rough times in China, and there was talk of furloughs and even retirements.

In the summer of 1929, Reverend J.D. Liddell was informed by the London Missionary Society that he would be retired and not returned to China. The years had taken a severe toll upon his health, especially the travels in the interior during his early years. Conditions were too unstable to return a man of his age to the field. So Eric's mother and father, sister, and brother Ernest sailed for Britain on the German liner *Saarbrucken* after emotional farewells.

Upon arrival in Scotland, they took a house in Edinburgh. There they were surrounded by old friends and people who told them about their famous son. On holidays they visited their relatives in Drymen. Reverend J.D. and Mrs. Liddell had made a spiritual and personal investment in the people of China which could scarcely be measured in human terms. While Eric would see them again in Scotland on his own furlough, his parents never returned to China. Jenny went home to a long, happy marriage with Dr. Charles Somerville who, by pure coincidence, also had served some time in the China mission field. Ernest finished his schooling and became a bank officer in Edinburgh.

At the graduation ceremony for the class of 1930 at TACC, the retirement of Dr. Lavington Hart was announced. This man was another towering giant of the missionary service. A Chinese educator was selected as the new principal, in keeping with the London Missionary Society's policy of trying to prepare China for eventual autonomy and assumption of Chinese authority over all functions. And this policy, of course, completely puts to rest the lie that the missionaries were feathering their own nests to remain forever in the foreign treaty enclaves.

After Eric's parents had left for Scotland, he moved into an apartment at the TACC with several medical and teaching colleagues. These men later would write memoirs that told of Eric's modesty, his genuineness, his hard work.

In the winter of 1930, Eric competed in the North China Athletics Championship. He won some events, but records of the meet do not survive. He worked diligently in his mission work, counseling with boys for long hours after classes were over, trying with every means at his command to teach, inspire, and convert.

Meanwhile, Eric had begun to cultivate a very special relationship with Florence Mackenzie, daughter of Mr. and Mrs. Hugh Mackenzie. In the summer of 1929 several missionary families organized a field trip to climb a high mountain where a famous Chinese religious hermit had stayed for years. Florence was seventeen and Eric was twenty-seven. On this outing they acknowledged their developing affection for one another. Eric was shy and circumspect around young women; and Florence, while young, possessed a strong personality. Their courtship on this trip was evidently a delight of little events amid the company of the missionaries, who camped for several nights on the outing. Perhaps Eric was trying to impress Florence a bit. They all stopped to rest after a particularly arduous climbing session, and Eric seemed to have disappeared. Suddenly they saw him well up on the next slope, barely visible in the mist and practically running. It appears that the entire family on both sides supported this courtship, which was to be drawn out by the circumstances of missionary life as it had been for both of their parents. Jenny sent an engagement ring, ordered by Eric, to Tientsin via a missionary friend. When it arrived, Eric made a shy proposal, Florence accepted, and the engagement was announced in the English newspaper.

Florence and her sister Margaret sailed for Canada in 1930, Florence to train as a nurse, and Margaret to attend university. Eric spent a lonely year, indeed, with his family and his fiancée in various distant lands.

Finally, in May of 1931, the Glasgow Students' Evangelical Union received notice that Eric was coming home on missionary furlough. A series of deputation appearances was planned, and Eric was elected in absentia as president of the Former Members' Fellowship.

The Chinese government under Chiang Kai-shek at Nanking announced its pro-Western "Educative Policy" at about the same time. Mao Tse-tung proclaimed the principles of the People's Revolution and organized the Red Army. Chiang Kai-shek would claim to have caught and eliminated the Red Army and Mao several times, but eventually would fall to the revolution himself.

None of this was imaginable to the missionaries in 1931. But Eric had a view of what was going on in another Asian power when he sailed eastward from Tientsin for home, via the Canadian route, on July 31, 1931. A fellow passenger on the liner was a Japanese evangelist named

Toyohiko Kagawa. He and Eric discussed at great length the possibilities for Christian influence to avert the impending military and revolutionary clashes that were sweeping the Orient. And Eric learned about Japanese athletes who were preparing to make their country a force in the upcoming 1932 Olympics at Los Angeles.

Eric and Florence had a joyous reunion at Toronto, following his long train ride across Canada. They agreed that Eric would take this route back to China after his furlough in Scotland, and that way they could see each other again before the long separation while Florence finished up her nurse's program. From Toronto, he went by train to Halifax, and on by steamer to Liverpool.

On August 31, 1931, Eric Liddell got off the train at the Waverley Station, six years and two months after the wild departure following his Olympic triumph. This time his parents, Jenny, and Ernest were present. So were his friends from the GSEU, his college and athletics friends, and many in Edinburgh who felt as strongly about him as when he lived there, such as Elsa McKechnie who had maintained her Eric Liddell fan club. People noticed that he looked lean and trim, bronzed by the searing sun of northeast China, and a bit older. His hairline had receded quite a lot, but his smile and his twinkling blue eyes were still the same. In his suitcase was a flowered shirt from Hawaii, popularized by fellow 1924 Olympics star Duke Kahanamoku.

There was a *Scottish Congregationalist* bulletin published in August stating that Eric would take two terms of study at the Scottish Congregational College, 29 Hope Terrace, following which he would be ordained. Then, a schedule of deputation appearances was announced that made the reader wonder how he was going to attend classes, or even see his parents in their Edinburgh home. Eric was no longer competing for medals, but he certainly had not slowed down.

*T*he *Reverend James D. Liddell* had done deputation work during the furloughs from China as long as Eric could remember, and now it was Eric's turn. On September 30, 1931, Eric spoke before a packed congregation at St. George's West Church in Edinburgh. Appearing with him was a row of well-known personalities from Scottish athletics and the student evangelical movement. People knew that things were bad in China, and Eric did not take long to get right to the point:

> I want to leave a message with you. We are all missionaries. We carry our religion with us, or we allow our religion to carry us. Wherever we go, we either bring people nearer to Christ, or we repel them from Christ. We are working for the great Kingdom of God—the time when all people will turn to Christ as their leader, and we will not be afraid to own Him as such.

Then he went to Glasgow for a huge service at the Renfield Street Church, the scene of his final triumph in the city in 1925. The welcome was thunderous, and Eric was invited to join in with several famous evangelists at the Annual Temperance Rally at the Church of Scotland Presbytery of Glasgow. He showed that he had not forgotten the problems of everyday life in Scotland when he told them:

> Two of the greatest problems the Church has to face are betting and gambling, and intemperance. These evils are sapping the energy of our young people, and the Church has to put up a united front against them, or they are bound to lose ground.

109

> Drink takes away from a man all that is honorable. One of the greatest athletes Scotland has ever produced, whom hundreds went to see, ended his days through drink by begging at the place where he used to be cheered. It is people who go down like that who present a challenge to old and young in their churches to see that the curse of drink is taken away from their glorious land.

In October, he made the circuit of churches and meeting halls on the entire belt of cities and towns between Edinburgh and Glasgow, and westward to the coastal towns beyond Glasgow. He made some progress in his divinity studies and visited his family as much as he could. Regular letters went across the Atlantic Ocean to Toronto, Canada.

In November he delighted his father by appearing in the family home village at Drymen. His message was sociological as he told how old customs and old reliances upon family were deteriorating in China. In their place was coming a new nationalism with opportunities for China to progress. Christians, however, must fill the void. The next night he spoke at the Women's Rural Institute, giving a remarkable exposition of Chinese history that made the ancient land sound positive and attractive.

In Belfast, Ireland he gave a report on the Tientsin Anglo Chinese College where he worked. He told how 10% of the five hundred students were boarders, and how football (soccer) was catching on. He gave them a picture of organized school sports in the Orient. All of his examples were stated in British terms instead of trying to dazzle the crowd with foreign expertise, and the Irish listeners were fascinated. He also gave the rationale behind his own commitment to education in the missionary service. "It is very hard to build up a church for people who have no literature, where 80 percent are illiterate. The educationalist," he said, "must follow on with the evangelist."

But then he took on another topic in Belfast that held a high emotional level of interest right at home—nationalism. "Chinese public opinion holds," he said, "that other nations have taken from her what should be hers, and they ask that the Concessions (treaty ports) which have been taken be returned. Without going too deeply into the politics of the matter, I think it would be extremely difficult to give the Concessions back all at once, but the policy is to hand them over gradually. The college at which I teach is in one of the Concessions, and it has not gone through the same troubles that many of the colleges had."

Eric surprised the Rotary Club back home at Stirling, for he portrayed the august Dr. Sun Yat-Sen, the leader of the revolutionaries who overthrew the Manchu government, as an anti-Western rabble rouser. He told them how the missionaries were trying to portray the spirit of sacrifice and kindliness in their relations with all of the Chinese people because they believe these things are the law of life.

In the days before Christmas, Eric made a tour of the Scottish border towns. These were rugby strongholds—Gala, Kelso, Melrose, Selkirk, and Jedburgh—and the men from the local rugby clubs sponsored rallies and church services. Most of them had a story or a memory to share from the days when Eric was in town with the Edinburgh XV for a match, and these towns also produced generous public contributions to support the work of the London Missionary Society.

Rob and his wife came home from China for Jenny's wedding that spring to Dr. Charles Somerville, the last time they would all be together. The Liddell family spent Christmas together, perhaps suspecting that there would not be many more. In January 1932, Eric began his final study term at the Scottish Congregational College, the last formal academic work he would take.

In March several big names from the world of sports came together at a service in Edinburgh. Eric was among them to endorse publicly a resolution to condemn sporting events held on Sunday. People who ever wondered if Eric regretted his decision to pass up additional Olympic medals in the relays, or possibly in the 100-meter race, had their answer. He regretted only the disappointment that some Scots felt over the matter, and also that a few people had difficulty understanding the absolute certainty and sincerity of his decision.

It was not until after Eric's death that another action of his ministry became known when a minister with whom he had visited during the January campaign wrote to Reverend D.P. Thomson. As Eric was leaving the church following the service, he signed the visitor's register. Below his name he drew in some Chinese characters with their translation in English: "Keep smiling." The minister told Eric that a woman named Bella in his congregation would be thrilled to see the autograph and inscription. She would barely be able to read it, however. Five years before she had suffered an industrial accident, blinding one eye and weakening the other. Her hearing was nearly gone, she had painful skin graft areas on her face, and she suffered from staggering headaches. Yet she remained cheerful and even managed to keep a home for four family members. The minister thought she would take Eric's little message as a personal word of cheer.

"But," said Eric, "I'd like to meet her. Would she mind?"

"Would she mind!" exclaimed the minister. "She would love it."

So Eric delayed his plans and went to spend an hour or so with this courageous soul named Bella. And several days later, Eric received a long, painfully scrawled letter from her, telling how she felt that God was using her and her affliction as a way to help others. This letter arrived at the address in Edinburgh where Eric's parents lived in retirement, and Eric was just leaving for a speaking engagement in London. He took the letter and read it on the train.

British trains in those days had rows of little compartments, each with two seats facing each other, and a side-opening door. There was only one companion in Eric's compartment on the trip to London, a young man who was utterly dejected. Eric drew this fellow into conversation and discovered that the man was actually contemplating suicide because of a series of adversities. No matter what words of hope, of God's love, that Eric might offer, the man simply would not be consoled. Eric felt frustrated until he remembered the letter in his pocket. Impulsively, he thrust it out.

"Here," he said, "read this."

The young man scanned the faint words scrawled on the sheets in the moving light of a jolting train compartment. Eric waited until he finished and then gently outlined the woman's condition. And before long, he got to the faith that was the reason for Bella's ability to see her plight as a gift. The young man's demeanor altered considerably, and he finally made the decision not to end his life.

As spring approached, so too did Eric's ordination as a minister. He was invited to several socials for the clergy, and his mother worried about dressing him up a bit. So she was appalled when he started out for an august meeting one warm day wearing his flowered Hawaiian shirt.

"Eric, you're part of the clergy now," said Mary Liddell.

"Yes Mother, and this shirt's worn by a duke," he reassured her, eyes twinkling.

But Eric switched the Duke Kohanamoky shirt for a proper suit, for the sartorial gems of a Hawaiian duke meant little to the Edinburgh clergy.

On June 22, 1932, Eric Liddell was ordained as a minister in the Chapel of the Scottish Congregational College. While most of Eric's residences, churches, and school buildings in Edinburgh are still extant in 1987, the lovely old mansion that housed the College was demolished just before Christmas of 1983. With ordination, Eric had now followed every part of his father's career save one, a rural pastorate in China among the peasant villages.

Emotions were strong as Eric sailed to Canada, for this time his mother and father would not be going out again. Everyone was proud of Eric, but there was sadness at the parting of this close-knit family. Jenny had her life in Bonnyrigg, near Edinburgh, and Ernest was attending an Edinburgh business college. Rob and his family again would be a short distance from Eric at the Siaochang mission.

At the Waverley Station, there were some tears. Mary Liddell still knew a few things about missionary life.

"Out in China, you know, we dreaded the long good-byes. So as not to cry, we made them joyful."

"And how was that, Mother?" asked Eric, knowing he would not see his parents again until 1939.

"We always said, 'Those who love God never meet for the last time.' That made it a meeting, not a parting." And they all smiled.

In Toronto, Eric and Florence discussed plans for their future. It would be some eighteen months before Florence finished up her nursing studies and came out to China for their wedding. The Toronto press was busy interviewing members of the British Olympic team, who were on their way to the Xth Olympiad in Los Angeles. Eric, because of his past Olympic honors, was interviewed by Mr. R.E. Knowles, who talked in all sorts of metaphors drawn from the classics and the sports field.

Knowles wanted to know about the big track meet in Port Arthur where Eric had tied the Olympic performances in the 200- and 400-meters events at Amsterdam with little preparation. Eric explained a little of the situation, then offered, "And it happened, somehow, that I won."

Knowles pressed on, seeking to have Eric say that the London Missionary Society authorities would not let him compete in the 1928 Games at Amsterdam.

"Did the missionary authorities instruct you to moderate your pace?" he asked, a lame bit of track talk meaning, "Did they tell you to quit running in big track meets?"

"Oh, no," said Eric.

"Had you their permission to compete?" persisted Knowles.

"Oh, no," replied Eric, leaving off, of course, the other pertinent fact that he never asked for any such permission.

Then came a question couched in terms so trite that it drew out the twinkle in Eric's eye.

"Do you think your pedal prowess is a help to you in your work?" asked Knowles, not knowing that Eric pedaled a bicycle all over Tientsin and the surrounding countryside.

"Sure," said Eric.

"Do you preach from the text, 'So run that ye may obtain?' "persisted Knowles, scarcely realizing that his citation of 1 Corinthians 9:24 was opening the door to a pair of theological gems.

"No, I'd sooner preach on, 'The race is not to the swift,' " said the missionary from China, where running was not popular.

Knowles retreated to safer ground about Eric's race agaisnt Dr. Otto Peltzer from Germany, who shortly would finish outside the final heat in the 1,500-meter event at Los Angeles. Eric gave generous replies about Peltzer, especially pointing out that Peltzer would compete at Los Angeles at the age of 32, when he, Eric, considered himself over the hill at thirty. Then Knowles did a theological encore.

"Are you glad you gave your life to missionary work? Don't you miss the limelight, the rush, the frenzy, the cheers, the rich red wine of victory?" he asked. It was common knowledge the Eric despised "limelight, rush and frenzy," and that he preached publicly against drinking alcoholic beverages.

If Knowles had been at a youth rally in Dundee, Scotland, the previous month he would have heard Eric refer to the writing of the Apostle Paul, who equated athletic competition with Christian striving. Eric told the packed audience, "It is not sufficient to admire Christ; it is not sufficient to love Him. 'For me to live is Christ,' cried the Apostle. That is the spirit in which work for God has to be done." This would

114

have been the answer for Mr. Knowles. But Eric gave a considerate reply to this loaded question.

"Oh, well, of course," Eric told Mr. Knowles, "it's natural for a chap to think over all that sometimes, but I'm glad I'm at the work I'm engaged in now. A fellow's life counts for far more at this than the other." Then he refered to St. Paul at Corinth, where the Apostle labored during the Isthmian Games of A.D. 50. "Not a corruptible crown, but an incorruptible, you know!" Eric knew that the oleaster leaves put on his head at McEwan Hall and the gold medal from Paris mattered nothing in comparison with the salvation of one illiterate peasant in the Hopei Province.

He said his good-byes to Florence and took the long train ride to the West Coast; from there he traveled by steamer to Hawaii, Japan, and China. The newspapers at each stop were full of news about the Olympic Games at Los Angeles in early August. Sandy McCloud Wright finished just out of the medals in the marathon. One Japanese athlete was Army Lieutenant Takeichi, Baron Nishi. He won the gold medal in the Prix de Nations, the glamorous jumping event of equestrianship, and was a big hit with silent screen stars Mary Pickford and Douglas Fairbanks, the athletics aficionados who had encouraged Charley Paddock to hang in and run the 200-meter race against Eric at Paris. What made the Baron Nishi unusual was that he was a career officer of the Imperial Army, and he expressed hope for world peace in the spirit of the Olympic movement, echoing the sentiments that Japanese evangelist Toyohiko Kagawa had discussed with Eric at the start of his furlough.

Rob Liddell and Annie Buchan were on duty down at Siaochang when Eric returned to Tientsin. Annie had been home in Peterhead, Scotland on her furlough at about the same time Eric was home. She had returned to China with her personal luggage crammed with donated quilts and linens for the Medical Mission. Things seemed to be going well at Siaochang, but the retirement of James Liddell and Dr. Lavington Hart from the TACC, and the murder of a teaching colleague, had made a great impact on how things were run at the college. So the newly-ordained Reverend Eric H. Liddell was assigned a much heavier load of duties, both at the TACC and at the Union Church. As his mother had come out to join his father in marriage, so Florence would come out for the wedding. But there would be little free time to count the days until she arrived.

T here is a rule in organizational affairs that the person who gets the work done will be given more opportunities to do more work! Eric Liddell had developed the Min Yuan Sports Field at the Tientsin Anglo-Chinese College, and in September of 1932 he was made Chairman of the Games Committee. In addition, he took over the position of Secretary of the College from his old teacher and colleague A.P. Cullen. This meant he did the correspondence and kept the records for the five hundred students and thirty faculty members.

It was a propitious time for education, apparently, in northeast China. Miss Annie Buchan reported upon her return in 1932 that "the new Governor had discouraged idol worship . . . when I arrived in Tientsin . . . the Chinese carried themselves with a bearing, but there was an obvious difference in their clothing. They were better paid and better fed, and that also combined to give out an air of respectability."

Nevertheless, fear of Japan's future intentions was also part of the daily conversation. In 1931 the Japanese government had taken advantage of the so-called "Mukden incident" to seize Manchuria. The Japanese Kwantung Army invented a Chinese plot to blow up the Port Arthur-Mukden Railroad, which gave them a pretext to seize first Mukden and then the entire district. In 1932 they proclaimed this region an autonomous province named Manchukuo. The Kwantung Army was permanently established there, which at times made policies of its own, almost as if the subjected province of China were an independent country. In 1933 this Kwantung Army cut off the Jehol Province that had functioned for a while as a kind of buffer state. The western maritime powers in the Orient seemed curiously disinterested in stopping Japanese aggression.

While Eric had been on furlough he made many new friends among the youth in Scotland. This reminded him of how the newsletter from the TACC had inspired him about the China missionary service during his school days at Eltham College. So he started his own column in the London Missionary Society Magazine.

In one article, telling about the construction of a building, he described how the Chinese laborers marched along in rows tamping the foundation mix into place with poles, or pulling a tamping weight up into the air by hauling on long cords from both sides and letting the weight fall free. All of this coordinated nicely, he reported, because the workers sang to set the rhythm and give the cues. "The singing made their day brighter and their work lighter," wrote Eric. "Have you ever tried it as you go about *your* work? And do you know the Saviour who puts a song into our hearts?"

Eric also told his readers about the Chinese love for songbirds. While these birds were kept as pets, and were appreciated by the Chinese, dogs were mistreated. Eric expressed hope for change when he wrote, "It is the gospel of Jesus Christ that has brought kindness to animals in China, till the same gospel enters into the hearts and minds of the people there." He described how hard the daily life was for people in China and told some dramatic stories about how Chinese Christians had performed beautiful, humanitarian acts.

About the same time, Eric exhibited his theological open-mindedness when Muriel Lester passed through Tientsin on a visit. She was the British associate of Mohandas K. (Mahatma) Gandhi, the Hindu nationalist leader in British India. While Gandhi is today an established figure in the religious opposition to repression through non-violent resistance, to many people living in the 1930s he was simply a rebel and disrupter of the British Empire. Muriel spoke on prayer at the Union Church. "Her face was so calm and joyous. . . ." reported Eric. "She's full of courage, and not that pugnacious kind which is not very admirable, but a noble, polished courage, which just knows and therefore does."

Eric did not commit to writing a fully developed theory of social action against injustice, and did not adapt Gandhi's thinking to the Christian political situation as did Dietrich Bonhoeffer in Germany or Martin Luther King, Jr. in America. But the concept was one that all missionaries wrestled with, and, after ministering among the Chinese during the Japanese military occupation that was to come, Eric would state his own beliefs about unearned suffering and its redemptive properties.

On Remembrance Day, 1933, far away in Edinburgh, it was the fifteenth anniversary of that day when the guns fell silent on the Western Front and World War I ended. A band of bagpipers led a unit of soldiers down the Castlehill Lawn from Edinburgh Castle to the square in front of the City Chambers, just opposite St. Giles Cathedral. They played the "Flowers of the Forest" at the slow-step, just as Eric had heard them do nine years before in Paris. As a lone bagpiper intoned a dirge from his spot on a tower of St. Giles, veterans of the World War laid wreaths on the Soldiers' Memorial.

Halfway around the world, Eric was preaching at the Union Church in Tientsin, as the Reverend J.D. Liddell often had done. That Sunday, Eric felt unusually close to his father, who was visiting the family home in Drymen. James D. Liddell sat down for a short nap in his chair; he had not been in good health. His sister came in to see if he needed anything, but found that he had slipped quietly away.

The telegram reached Eric in China the next morning as he was finishing his breakfast. He thought of the love, the sacrifice, the service his father had poured into missionary work in China; how he had modeled his own life upon that treasure that was his father's career. No one knew how many Chinese farmers in the rural areas had received the loving touch of this Christian servant. He heard the call to China in a town in Scotland, committed his life to it, and transmitted the call to his children. No greater eulogy was required. Eric received a final letter from his father two weeks later, and it was conveyed to him that his father was "full of energy" on the day preceding his death.

In January, Eric was hard at work with his baptismal counseling, his science classes, and the college's recordkeeping. But he found time to write to his mother frequently after his father died. He knew she would be interested in his plans for the wedding and in keeping up with the daily events of his life in missionary service. He said it would be "Jen's white furniture for our bedroom," and he was using other family pieces and locally discovered bargains to furnish a nice home. The missionaries had little money to spend, and yet they were adept at keeping immaculate homes that probably made foreign visitors exaggerate their affluence.

He wrote his mother about how pleased he was that she had looked up his favorite hymn, which he had described in an earlier letter. The tune was Jean Sibelius's musical tribute to his homeland, *Finlandia;* the words told so much about Eric Liddell. "Be still my soul, the Lord is on thy side," it went, and Eric thought the tune was "calm, restful, beautiful" when he played it for himself on the piano.

Florence passed her final nursing examinations in late November at Toronto General Hosptial. She would perform general hospital duties until January of 1934. Eric had his mind on their impending wedding now, for in the first week of December 1933, he got the apartment where they would live cleaned up and painted. Florence had written that she and her mother would sail for China from Vancouver aboard the *Empress of Canada* on February 10, 1934.

On January 31, Florence and Mrs. Mackenzie left Toronto to begin the long journey. Eric showed how much his mind was on Chinese ways of thinking by writing letters that referred to months as "moon," an English translation for the Chinese word. Li Mu Shi, as Eric was called in Chinese, was working steadily on his Chinese language skills. In the weeks before Florence arrived, he baptized a number of his Sunday school boys. He had also been in China long enough now to have some graduates. In February he was delighted to receive a visit from some of his alumni, and also from some men who had been baptized by his father years before.

Eric had carried the idea of the student athletes' evangelical system with him to China. Those who heard him speak for the GSEU with D.P. Thomson in Scotland probably did not fully grasp the extent to which Eric saw all of this as preparation for his missionary call to China. His Min Yuan Sports Field was the facility for training Christians, not just a place to have games. For him, teaching science and literacy was designed to prepare minds to receive Christian instruction and values, not just a job or an intellectual challenge. In the weeks before

Florence arrived for their wedding, he threw himself wholly into getting his Chinese version of the student-athlete-Christian alliance organized and functioning regularly.

Early in March, Eric was moving things into the house that he and Florence would occupy. He unpacked the medals and cups, some of which had been put away for years. That month he also was involved in the intricacies of school administration, trying to untangle college exams and board of education policy requirements. Perhaps he was homesick that month, for he wrote to his mother that she ought to go out to Jenny's house and see the snowdrops, crocuses, and daffodils in his sister's garden. On furlough, he had seen both the house where his mother lived and the Somerville home where Jenny lived. Eric could easily picture his beloved mother and sister there together in the garden.

On Tuesday, March 6, he went down to Taku for the arrival of the *Empress of Canada*. A strong offshore wind dropped the water level in the harbor so that the ship could not dock. Eric spent long hours waiting with his future father-in-law, hanging upon every scrap of information from the harbor master about when the ship would finally arrive. When it finally did, Eric and Florence sat up most of the night talking, catching up on events in each other's lives, and making plans. They rolled their wedding date back by four days in order to take advantage of a holiday at the TACC, thereby giving the young couple time for a honeymoon.

The marriage service at the Union Church on March 27, 1934, was jammed with both Chinese and European guests. The Liddells and the Mackenzies were two of the founding pillars of the Tientsin missionary community. The Reverend Ernest Richards, an old colleague of Eric's father, performed the service, assisted by Dr. Murdock Mackenzie, a forty-three year China veteran and the man who had baptized Florence. (The similarity in name is coincidental, as Florence often explained to visitors.) Mr. Hugh Mackenzie gave his daughter away, and Florence's bridesmaid was her friend Miss Gwyneth Rees. Florence's wedding dress was the one in which her mother was married, and Jenny had worn the same veil at the altar in Edinburgh when she married Dr. Charles Somerville.

These missionary people were accustomed to long family separations on opposite sides of the world, but they knew how to tie their families together, spiritually and symbolically. The wedding was unusually beautiful, in a more leisurely, stately era when people put personal attention into the details of the nuptials. The one luxury that Eric and Florence would ever have, following Mr. and Mrs. Hugh Mackenzie's wedding reception at 70 Cambridge Road, was a honeymoon at the Western Hill Hotel in Peking.

It was the family training and commitment for the missionary service that was the basis of life for both Florence and Eric. What they lacked in time together and in experience at making homes, they more than made up in personal commitment to what they were doing. They had powerful role models in their four parents, who had carved a niche for their children of cultured European life in China out of tough surroundings. Florence and Eric both had strong personalities, but they also each had a spirit of humility, of commitment to making their marriage and their missionary service a success. They were both motivated and guided by God's will in every detail of life, and they both had a rich sense of humor that eased difficult circumstances.

Shortly after Eric and Florence took up married life at the London Missionary Society compound, things deteriorated politically. The Chinese Communist Party formed a revolutionary army which Mao Tse-tung led on the famous "Long March." Eventually, Mao established a headquarters in remote Yenan. The Japanese forces were threatening to burst out of Manchuria. Small wonder that Rob and Annie, down at Siaochang, found the Chinese Eighth Route Army troops everywhere. And Eric was forced to come to terms with compulsory military cadet drills for his students at the TACC.

Though Eric attended Eltham College during the greatest war in history, he did not participate in a cadet program because of the small size of the student body. It is ironic that he then had military drill imposed on his missionary college students in China. "By orders from the government," Eric wrote in December of 1934, "one of our classes has to take military drill, and although I hate war, and feel the attitude of Christian people to it is going to be one of the greatest challenges in the future, yet [the drill] has smartened up some of the lads quite a bit."

During the same period, Eric organized a voluntary breakfast prayer group among the TACC staff. This was a time that required a great deal of spiritual strength for the Chinese and those dwelling in their land.

In 1935, Japanese troops penetrated across the Great Wall of China, north of Peking, biting off the Chahar Province. Similar encroachments were going on in Europe, too, where Berlin was preparing to host the XIth Olympiad in 1936, and Adolf Hitler was planning to convert the lovely Olympic pageantry into a mixture of historical symbolism and ugly Nazi propaganda.

In June of 1935, Florence was expecting their first child and went a bit earlier than usual to the beach retreat at Pei-tei-ho. Eric went to visit her there, and both came down with a bad case of influenza, which was a serious matter for expecting mothers in those days before antibiotics. Eric's reason for going to see Florence at Pei-tai-ho before the usual missionary staff holiday was that a tough career choice had been put to him.

The District Council of the London Missionary Society took notice in early 1935 that their rural stations were badly understaffed. Further, the operation was tougher to maintain now in the interior. So Eric was asked if he would give up his teaching at the college and go out to the Siaochang station with Florence, where Rob lived with his wife. After extensive prayer, Eric asked not to be transferred. He felt that his language skills were too weak for rural pastoral work, and that his science teaching was an asset that would not easily be replaced. But the decision was troubling for him. There is no evidence of criticism from his superiors over the fact that he asked not to be reassigned in 1935.

On July 13, 1935, Florence gave birth to their daughter Patricia at the Mackenzie Hospital in Tientsin. The *amah* tradition had changed a lot since Eric and Florence were babies in China. There were Chinese nursemaids, but their feet were not bound, and they came in only during the day for work. Eric and Florence were warm, loving parents; Patricia would become the only one of Eric's three children who had any real memories of their father.

The school year 1935-1936 brought still more pressure on Eric, because the boys at TACC were being pressured to perform military service, and Eric was hearing from Rob and other missionaries about the great needs in the rural zones. In March 1936, Joseph Stalin of the Soviet Union promised to come to the aid of China if the Japanese should encroach any farther, but it was a hollow promise. The Japanese military machine seemed to be moving closer and closer, and there were chilling stories about the things they did in the provinces where their troops were in control.

In July of 1936, the District Council decided that Eric should perform a four-month trial assignment as a rural missionary, working out of Siaochang. The choice, thereafter, would be his. He and Florence took little Patricia to Pei-tai-ho in August. Eric was delighted that Patricia could walk already, and there were the expected jokes from other adults that she would some day run faster than her father.

In the fall, Eric left his wife and baby for the first time on a provisional assignment as a rural pastor. He was shocked at how hard life was, not only from natural occurrences like droughts, floods, and crop pestilences, but from internal political struggles as well.

Farther north, Japanese Major General Kenji Doihara announced a plan to carve another autonomous province out of China, this one to consist of Chahar, Suiyan, Shansi, Hopei, and Shantung. The Hopei Province happened to be the area where Tientsin and Siaochang were located, and although his plan was a trial balloon at the time, it made Japanese intentions quite clear.

In late 1936, Chiang Kai-shek was nearly overthrown by a clique in his own government who demanded that he cease the struggle against the Communists internally, and unite all forces in China to fight and evict the Japanese. American General Joe Stilwell would take the same position in his role as theater commander in the years to come, and the matter would become one of the most acrimonious debates in modern Oriental history.

On January 6, 1937, Florence gave birth to their second daughter, Heather. They went to Pei-tai-ho for the summer vacation, but this time it was their last period together before a drastic change in their lives. That spring, the question that had come up the previous year about his future in China had been decided: Eric would become a rural pastor, working out of Siaochang. And it was deemed too dangerous for Florence, with two young babies, to move with him because of the banditry, the political fighting, and the almost certain invasion of the Japanese.

Eric would have thought it too dramatic in August of 1937 to say that he was being called "to Calvary," but that in a sense was the way it would be, and Miss Annie Buchan said it best. "Chinese and foreigners had endured the lean years of war, flood, and famine, and were just at the dawn of hope in 1937 when the Japanese declared war on China, and our good times were short-lived."

So as 1937 was drawing to a close, Eric was working out of Siaochang, where he had been a little boy and where Rob and Annie now ran the hospital. He would see Florence, Patricia, and little Heather a few days out of each month on hurried visits. And he would see daily acts of such violence and human depravity that it would tax all the resources of his athletic body, his deep faith, and his long training.

T here was a sign over the gate at Siaochang that read: *Chung, Wai, I Chai* (Chinese and Foreigners, All One Home). It was put up when the mission was reconstructed after the Boxer Rebellion. But that ironic message, along with all of Siaochang, was completely destroyed during the Japanese occupation in World War II. Today, a visitor would not be able to find even the building foundations of the mission station where Eric Liddell was a young boy, and out of which he worked as a rural missionary for two years. There had been four dwelling houses, the big church, the women's dormitory, and the girls' boarding school.

From mid-1937 until early 1940, when the Japanese district commander ordered the missionaries to evacuate the facility, it performed a Christian rescue and mercy mission to over twenty thousand resident victims, and a field outreach mission to tens of thousands more in facilities designed at the turn of the century for a few hundred at most!

Rob, Eric, Annie Buchan, and one or two additional Western missionaries were the entire organizational force of this remarkable effort. They worked tirelessly, amid constant fear and danger, with a dedicated staff of Chinese Christians trained right in the district. It was not easy for Eric to give up his work at the TACC, where he was so effective and so unique in his several teaching and pastoral roles. Nor was it pleasant to leave Florence, Patricia, and Heather in Tientsin.

"There were friends," said Florence, "on both sides of the question (either to go to Siaochang or stay at the TACC) who felt very strongly about it. However, after much prayerful consideration . . . he felt God was calling him to the country, and I think it was quite obvious he did the right thing. He loved the work, his health improved, and I think he blossomed out in a new way." It could also be pointed out that Eric had a courageous wife, steeped in the values of the China missionary service, who was willing to stay at Tientsin and care for the children, never knowing if her husband would come back alive after each visit.

Eric enjoyed his time with Patricia, writing about little details of her development to friends in Scotland. He rigged up a seat on the handlebars of his bicycle so she could go around the compound with him and even to a limited degree in the streets, which were full of soldiers. The staff and students at the TACC also missed Eric when he went into the field. "To say that we have missed him," stated the august annual report of the college, "not only in his Science teaching and in Athletics . . . would be to say the least that is possible." Eric undoubtedly appreciated this kind of simple mention, for he always said little and did much; and he despised foppish displays of gratitude, especially towards himself.

In 1937 it was noticed by some that Eric seemed to be influenced by the religious ideas of the American evangelist Frank Buchman. Buchman founded the "Oxford Group" which later took on a political orientation through Moral Re-Armament. It stressed four central absolutes: purity, honesty, love, and unselfishness. There was a requirement for a personal "quiet hour" with God, which Eric had done all his life anyway, and group discussion of one's personal spiritual shortcomings, which Eric did not like, either for himself or for others. There have been several similar happenings in British religious history. Eric was too direct, too much of a missionary activist, to spend much time splitting theological hairs, and so the influence of Buchmanism in his ministry is not central. It was simply a passing vehicle. And in that same year, Eric produced his own book of prayers that laid out his own theological viewpoint.

Eric Liddell's faith was based primarily upon the Beatitudes (Matthew 5:3-16), and the social gospel given by St. Paul in 1 Corinthians 13. The missionary work that carried these truths to people was founded upon 1 Corinthians 9:24-26. The symbolism of these verses is based upon the sporting analogy, which explains why Eric believed in the moral foundations of the Olympic Games, but also kept athletics in perspective as part of more important things. Because Eric did not write any long, scholarly treatises on theology, it has been said that he was not very intellectual. But this notion confuses intellectual trappings with real brilliance, for Eric's social applications of Christ's teachings stand on the winner's box.

He used an ecumenical, highly international aggregation of religious writings to illustrate his points; the breadth of his research coupled with his practical applications of moral teaching to the realities of life reveal a profound faith in God. His examples came from Aristotle, St. Elizabeth of Hungary, Mohandas K. Gandhi, Abraham Lincoln, David Livingstone, William Penn, James Hudson Taylor, and Booker T. Washington, to name a few. He showed moral and intellectual toughness by answering questions instead of evading them. Weakness and meekness, he said, are different. God demands the second and eschews the first, for weakness is based upon fear instead of faith. Eric offered hymns, stories, poems, and readings to go with his collection of lessons. Examples were given to illustrate each situation, drawing upon an actual decision or action. Any teacher of theology, any Sunday school teacher of an adult or of a youth class, would benefit from Eric's book *Reflections on the Sermon on the Mount.* Clearly, Eric's ability to teach so well did not depend upon being an Olympic athlete. Most of the Chinese students with whom Eric worked after 1925 did not have much understanding of his Olympic achievements; he had to make his own way as a teacher of religious principles, and his book of lessons shows how he did it.

Miss Annie Buchan noted, when Eric began working down at Siaochang, that the Chinese government was applying an old proverb to the political situation, and that the proverb also had a British counterpart. The British called the dilemma "biting off more than you can chew." The Chinese proverb called it "taking more in their mouths than they can swallow." The Japanese Army was technologically superior to the Chinese forces at any point where the Japanese were massed, but China had over seven hundred million people, millions of square miles, and a long history of absorbing and swallowing up militarily superior invaders.

Generalissimo Chiang Kai-shek rightly recognized that he could not beat the Communists in the interior and the Japanese along the seacoast simultaneously. So he worked with the Communists when he could, and adopted the Fabian tactics of guerrilla warfare against the Japanese, tactics that the Communists would use to defeat him and overthrow him after the Japanese finally surrendered in September 1945. This policy, in 1937, meant that Chinese Nationalist troops of the Eighth Route Army were stationed in detachments around the Hopei Province, hitting the Japanese a blow when they could, and trying to do it in a way that would not invite reprisals against the civilian population. While the missionaries supported Chiang Kai-shek as the best military force in a bad situation, they were aware that some of the units that were nominally from the Chinese Army were actually warlord elements, and that some were outright bandits. The Japanese Army often worsened its own situation by abusing citizens who would have remained passive.

Eric was welcomed enthusiastically at the Siaochang Hospital. His brother Rob was the Chief Surgeon, and people remembered his parents. He spent a day or two each week at Siaochang, and the rest of the time he pedaled his bicycle around the countryside, staying in the homes of Chinese Christians, organizing worship services and trying to relieve suffering when he could. He also worked on learning local dialects and medical first aid, since Rob was due for furlough in 1938 and no medical doctor was available to replace him. At Christmas 1937, Eric and Florence celebrated a grateful holiday with the girls at Tientsin, which also was under tension even though the Japanese did not yet dare to attack the European enclaves.

In the winter of 1938 the Japanese garrison unit at Siaochang initiated a campaign of petty persecution against the missionaries in the hope of driving them out. An officer would threaten and demand papers while soldiers searched their pockets. There was usually rifle fire or machine gun chatter audible from somewhere in the district. Eric became a legend at the practice of passive, non-violent resistance. He would smile, bow courteously, but not with the obsequiousness that the Japanese wanted from the Westerners to impress the Chinese. He tricked the Japanese guards at times by hiding money in his shoe, or by smuggling supplies for sick or hungry people under something in his mule cart; but he kept on the alert for Christians among the Japanese soldiers and occasionally found one who would allow him to do some decent act of service.

"It was a beautiful day [in February 1938]," reported Eric in a letter to Scotland, "when I started to wend my way to Ming Shih Chuang. The road is really quite all right if you get on to the right path, but so many paths are cut up that unless you have been over the course before, you get mixed up and find yourself carrying your bike over the trenches.

"At Ming Shih Chuang, I met the evangelist, Wang Feug Chou, who was to go with me. His home is in Nan Kung, so he knew the way. We started with a short prayer for guidance during the day."

Eric went on to tell how they met an old man at a carpenter's shop, where the workers seemed to be making an inordinate number of coffins. They saw the Japanese flag waving over Chuan Tyu. "The people in the village were busy spinning thread . . . the crops in Nan Kung have been largely a failure. . . . I stayed in the home of the father of one of the Siaochang School boys. . . . It was a large family of twenty . . . last year cholera carried away four."

Eric told how the Eighth Route Army was conscripting all the males below the age of forty-five. To enter each village the traveler had to be able to recognize two or three Chinese characters written on a signboard, a kind of code of population control. A Chinese cavalry unit was based in the district and took turns shaking the people down for food and money. Eric told about having dinner in the home of a poor family who took turns staying up all night spinning thread in order to make some money. Eric's hosts performed all the polite dining rituals as the pitiful meal was served, and then they all took turns singing hymns in Chinese and in English.

On this same trip, he came to a home where two widows lived together with their daughters. One of their husbands had been made an example and was shot by the Japanese because he had no ransom money to pay. "I bowed in the courtyard and asked God's blessing upon them," said Eric, "but the words seemed almost to come back, 'What could God do?' " This trip ended on a happier note when Eric learned that a man called Ma Fi Tun of Siaochang had just been released from five months' imprisonment, and they offered prayers of thanks.

Eric seemed to have found a God-given mission with this work. He showed endless patience, boundless sympathy, and love that simply gave and gave without question. "Eric's methods," reported Annie Buchan, "were . . . simple, clear, and direct. He lived a 'God-controlled life.' At Siaochang our preachers, nurses, and students hung on his words. Eric had the sympathy and the patience needed for work among a slow-moving people, whose 'hold-ups' by bandits and interference from soldiers were common occurrences; for preaching in all weathers . . . for dreary treks over the plain, or for wrestling with flood and famine."

In June 1938, Dr. Rob Liddell went home on furlough. It was hard for him to do, because he, too, was a missionary inspired with the same fervor as Eric. But he had been sick several times, and missionaries needed furloughs to remain effective. Eric laughed that "iodine and magnesium sulphate were the limit" of his medical knowledge, which was not really true, and so replaced his brother, becoming the Acting Superintendent of the Siaochang Hospital. The Japanese sent a mounted unit into the district and seized the railroad east of Siaochang. Thus, at Tehchow, where they had taken the ferry for years on the trip up to Tientsin, the missionaries now had to pass through Japanese military lines.

In July 1938, Eric took Florence and the girls up to Pei-tai-ho. Little Patricia could run along the sand as Eric and Rob had done when they were little boys there. They had a wonderful time, but Eric went back to Siaochang early because the only other missionary on duty there was due for furlough. The Eighth Route Army was utilizing guerrilla tactics, hitting the railroad, pulling up sections of track, inflicting casualties on the Japanese whenever they could. And after each attack, there would be the reprisals upon Chinese civilians. So Eric feared to bring Florence and the girls down to Siaochang.

An official from the London Missionary Society came out allegedly for an "inspection trip," but really to decide if it was time to pull out the operation. Their train ride south from Tientsin was interrupted by a guerrilla attack. The official noticed that Eric kept his money hidden in his shoe, so the official did the same. Eric told how he had tried to take a barge load of coal down the river to Siaochang a few days before, and had been robbed both by the Japanese and then by the Chinese troops!

Just before Christmas 1938, Eric went to a small village to conduct a baptism. There were only a few in the congregation. A military scouting airplane droned overhead. Eric kept on with the service, and the small congregation sang some hymns. Meanwhile, thirty-one truckloads of Japanese soldiers poured into the village. Their interpreter reassured everyone that civilians were in no danger, they were just here to fight the "bandits," which was the term they used to try to turn the Chinese against their own forces.

In this same village, Eric met a man who had once been a success in business but had become an opium addict. The man had become converted to Christianity when a Japanese unit rounded him up with some others, conducted a drumhead trial, and executed all but this man. "He had come home as quickly as he could," said Eric, "picked up a lantern from his house, and come on to the church. . . . We listened to him tell his story, and when it was finished we all rose together and thanked God."

Christmas with Florence and the girls that year was, Eric reported, "rich with memories of the Grace of God, which leads up confidently into another year knowing that His grace is sufficient for every need."

In January 1939, Eric left Siaochang to attend to his rural ministries; Miss Annie Buchan also was out of the mission station on a short holiday. When she returned, someone had pulled down the Japanese flag that replaced the Union Jack over the mission. And the Japanese flag had been replaced with the yellow lion on the yellow cross, over a blue field—the national colors of Scotland! The Japanese district officer was furious, but someone persuaded the officer that it was only "a joke on honorable Matron," so he joined in the laughter.

But the laughter did not last. Japanese forces carried out a major operation around Siaochang in mid-February, flooding the little station with wounded. Eric and Dr. Ken McCall came in to assist. On February 17, Eric was told about a wounded man who lay in a rural temple, apparently shot and left for dead by Japanese soldiers. He engaged a mule cart with driver and the next day rode his bicycle with the cart to Huo Chu, some eighteen miles from Siaochang. Eric rode on to Pei Lyn Tyu, three miles farther, to clear the matter with the village headman.

The wounded man had been unattended and left outdoors in the cold for five days; anyone who helped him would suffer death from the Japanese for interfering. A courageous friend had kept the man alive by smuggling food out to him, and he lay on a thin mattress, barely alive. Eric went to the village for the night, knowing that a Japanese motorized rifle company with a tank was in the next town. He prayed; he let his Chinese New Testament fall open and looked at Luke 16:10. "He that is faithful in that which is least is faithful also in much; and he that is unjust in the least is unjust also in much."

The next morning Eric and the mule driver started back to the little temple to pick up the wounded man. The Japanese motorized unit took a different turn and went away! When they came to the temple, some villagers crowded around and made it difficult to pick up the victim.

It was Chinese New Year and the people thought their burnt offerings might save the poor man, when Eric could see he was choking. So Eric gave a little impromptu sermon in Chinese about burnt offerings from the Book of Micah. He finally persuaded the people to let him load the sick man on the mule cart and leave. But then someone told Eric of another seriously wounded man in the nearby village of Pang Chuang. So the little procession went to that hamlet and saw another headman.

The second man lay inside a hut. He and five others had been taken out for execution by a Japanese military detachment. The men were made to kneel as a Japanese officer moved along the line, slicing their heads off with his saber. However, on the sixth victim, he missed, giving him a deep gash from behind the neck around to the side of his jaw, and the officer left him for dead. Eric explained to the family of this man that the mule cart already had one wounded person, but that they would carry him the remaining eighteen bumpy miles to the Siaochang Hospital tied to the shaft that connected the cart to the mule's yoke.

During the four-hour trip back, they were screened by a Japanese military reconnaissance plane, and they were told of a Japanese Army patrol shadowing them on a parallel route. But they made it back. The doctors sewed up the man with the saber slash and he recovered miraculously; the pitiful fellow from the temple died in two days. The man with the saber wound became a devout Christian during his convalescent sessions with Eric. And he turned out to be an artist. In gratitude, he painted several pictures, and one, a peony rose, was so good that Eric had it lithographed. The caption, in Chinese, translates, "The peony rose is the most beautiful in China. Her modesty and manner come from God."

This story was presented as a sermon in pulpits all over Scotland, and copies of the lithograph were sold to help support the work of the London Missionary Society in China. In July, Eric and Florence were sent on furlough. Germany and Russia were doing saber rattling that tended to put the news from China on the back burner. Indeed, the idyllic tropical life for British, French, and American garrisons all across the Pacific theater was scarcely disturbed except in China.

Eric Liddell must have known that the war would expand in Asia. Yet in July 1939, he said, "The flag is still flying, so don't get depressed. There is still plenty to thank God for." He and Florence started the long cruise across the Pacific, with a stop in Hawaii, and then to Vancouver. He could still laugh, but he had some serious things to tell people in Canada and Scotland.

*E*ach time Eric Liddell went to China, his arrival seemed to coincide with war and unheaval. He was born during the suppression campaigns against the Boxer Rebellion, returned after schooling in Britain to face the 1925 Shanghai uprising and the student revolts, and returned from his first furlough in time for the Japanese invasion of Manchuria and the internal struggles of 1932. Coming home for his second furlough in 1939, he was entering the arena for the start of World War II. For a man who hated war, it gave him ample opportunity to practice his superb skills as a peacemaker.

In March 1938, Adolf Hitler's army carried out the annexation of Austria, designed to make it appear as if Austria would prefer to be ruled from Berlin. It was the way things were done in the Orient sometimes when someone wanted the adjacent province or country. Hitler accomplished his operations in Austria so well that he followed on with the covert plan to conquer Czechoslovakia. In the last two days of September, Prime Minister A. Neville Chamberlain of Britain and Premier Edouard Daladier of France legitimized Germany's new prizes at Munich in exchange for a vague promise of future peace.

In May of 1939, as Eric and Florence were planning their furlough, Germany made a huge territorial demand upon Poland, and the very next day, May 22, came the famous Hitler-Mussolini "steel pact." In late August, Stalin, who had promised help to the Chinese if the Japanese should invade Manchuria, signed a non-aggression pact with Hitler over Poland. As Eric and Florence were arriving in Canada so the Mackenzies could meet their new granddaughters, Hitler's army was conquering the western half of Poland. Two weeks later the Soviet Union seized the eastern half.

In Toronto, conversations reflected the political concerns of Britain and America; while the Royal Navy still ruled the waves, there was great fear of German submarines. German U-boat skippers considered anything with the Union Jack to be fair game, so Eric and Florence discussed their future plans for travel. Maybe the thing to do was for Eric to go to Scotland alone; but then, of course, Mother, Jenny, and Ernest would not get to see Patricia and Heather. Again, Eric seemed to be put into situations where he had to give up something that was reasonable and worthy.

When he was preparing to leave on furlough, Miss Annie Buchan had asked him if he regretted giving up his teaching at the college to become a rural missionary. "Have you any regrets about leaving a city and a college with high-grade students and coming here, trudging 'round this district in all weathers?" It was the same sort of thing people asked him about giving up the Sunday events at Paris in 1924, and about not running at all in the 1928 Games at Amsterdam.

But he had told Miss Annie, "Never! I never had so much joy and freedom in my work as here." So in the spirit of being glad for what he did have, and feeling that he was doing the right thing for the safety of Florence and the girls, he went on to Scotland alone. The crossing was uneventful, and Eric was once again received as a hero in Edinburgh. He stayed with his mother at 120 Marchmont Road, and the news he had for her about Siaochang, where her memory was revered, was depressing to her, even in Eric's cheerful way of telling it. Reverend D.P. Thomson arranged several public appearances for Eric at churches; people noticed that he looked a good deal older and more serious.

The XIIth Olympiad had been scheduled by the International Olympic Organizing Committee for Tokyo in 1940, but the invitation was withdrawn after the invasion of China. It was reissued to Helsinki, Finland, where frantic efforts were under way to prepare a stadium, natatoria, and other venues. But on November 30, 1939, Stalin hurled the Soviet juggernaut at the incredibly brave Finnish Army, and the Games of 1940 were called off altogether.

Eric spent Christmas with his mother, Jenny and Charles, and Ernest, who was now training as a lieutenant of Royal Artillery. Eric wrote to the Royal Air Foce and volunteered his services as a pilot. They offered him a desk job instead, saying he was too old at thirty-seven. There can be little doubt that Eric Liddell, at the stick of a Spitfire in the Battle of Britain the following year, would have been as tough a combat pilot as he had been a three quarter wing in rugby. He had the athlete's sharp reflexes, natural balance and timing, and was in superb physical condition from cycling around the backlands of the Hopei Province. Could he have pulled the trigger on a German pilot? Probably not. But in retrospect, the Royal Air Force made a good decision; they produced a crop of heroes in the sky, and Eric Liddell was made for a different realm of knighthood, under a different sky.

A few days after Christmas, he wrote to Elsa McKechnie, offering congratulations upon her becoming Mrs. Watson. Her Eric Liddell fan club was a thing of the past now, but she had the premier collection of scrapbooks about his career. He told her how Florence and the girls were staying in Canada for this furlough because of the danger from the submarine "wolf packs," and that his days were filled with deputation work. He was enjoying "the dampness in the air" which was "very refreshing after the dryness of China."

Eric sent Elsa a lithograph copy of the peony rose painted by Li Hsin Sheng, the painter rescued by Eric after his head was nearly severed by a Japanese officer. One year later, the British government issued a request for metal, paper, and anything that citizens had that could be recycled industrially and converted into munitions. Impulsively, Elsa contributed her Eric Liddell scrapbooks, which were recycled to make cardboard, and the world's most complete collection of photographs, programs, and newspaper cuttings about Eric became boxes for the war effort. But in Elsa's drawing room today, the peony rose hangs on the wall, and you can look out the window into the neighborhood that has not changed much since Eric lived there and imagine him riding past on his bike as she talks about him.

During his 1932 furlough deputation appearances, Eric had shown the beginning of a skill to describe complex political situations in China in a way that was fair and sympathetic. Now, to the Rotary Club at Stirling, and before church groups, he displayed a sophisticated command of the complex, heart-breaking milieu in which he had been working. He told how the mechanized and better equipped Japanese forces were able to seize the railroads and ports, just as the French and British had done over the years. But the Chinese forces had retreated nearly a thousand miles, drawing the Japanese farther and farther into the populous interior. There, they used the hit-and-run tactics of guerrilla warfare, inflicting casualties and costing the Japanese military equipment that was the basis of their military superiority.

He explained how China had used her great population and her vast interior for centuries to absorb and eventually thwart aggressors. The Japanese were paying for the war by taking control of the narcotics trade, which had shifted from opium now to the more sophisticated heroin industry. Japanese administrators had seized the banks in the cities where they had military control, calling in the Chinese money and issuing their own occupation scrip at rates favorable, of course, to the occupying power. Universities were seen by the Japanese as a unifying patriotic force, and so thousands of Chinese students were fleeing to the south or serving in the armies. And pressure was being put on the English language newspapers that served the foreign enclaves at Peking and Tientsin.

In February 1940, the convoy system of the Royal Navy, with many forms of assistance short of armed engagement by the U.S. Navy and Coast Guard, was bringing some degree of safety to crossing the Atlantic. Eric and Florence decided that she should bring the girls across and, in March, Mary Liddell got to see her new grandchildren. They played with Jenny's two daughters. Rob had joined the Emergency Medical Service, and, Reverend James D. Liddell would have been delighted had he lived long enough to see all his grandchildren in Britain at the same time, even for a few months.

In the spring, Eric gave a talk in England at which several Chinese citizens were present in the audience. He spoke so naturally about the bizarre situation of invading soldiers, bandits, people living in near starvation conditions, and several kinds of contending Chinese forces, that the Chinese and the British leaders alike gained an artificially serene picture of what life was like at Siaochang. A later report by one of the Siaochang Mission medical staff revealed that the situation had stretched the missionaries to the limits of human tolerance, and that Eric's powerful spirit had been their source of stability. Over and over he had interfered gently to keep Japanese non-coms and officers from abusing people. He insisted always that they admit sick and wounded of all sides—Japanese, civilians, bandits, and Chinese combatants from the three distinct affiliations: Eighth Route Army, Nationalist, and Communist.

While Eric was explaining the situations in China, Hitler was laying plans for a cross-Channel invasion of Britain, and the East-West Axis alliance was signed between Germany, Italy, and Japan. Wang Ching-wei became the pro-Japanese puppet leader of China in occupied Nanking, joining the list of pro-Axis stooges who eventually became heads of state in Norway, France, and most of the countries overrun by the Axis forces. While the Liddells were engaging a cottage in the country for a last vacation together, Germany invaded Denmark and Norway. Denmark lasted a few hours, and Norway fell after six weeks.

After Florence and the girls arrived in Scotland, they were involved in a train collision that could have been a tragedy. They all gave thanks to God that no one was hurt. Mrs. Liddell wanted them to have time together in a vacation rental house, and so, that summer, they had delightful weeks without war and suffering right at hand.

"Mother and I were always grateful," Jenny recalls, "that we could give Eric, Florence, and the girls that little time together in the cottage."

They could all do nothing but grieve when the overrated French Maginot Line fell easily before the fast, powerfully armed Panzer divisions of the Wehrmacht, but they were all thankful that some 335,000 soldiers of the British Expeditionary Force were rescued on the beaches at Dunkirk by June 10, 1940. Dr. Rob Liddell was deeply involved in emergency medical work, and young Lieutenant Ernest Liddell was posted to an artillery unit.

On June 10, Italy invaded France from the south, when it was obvious they could not lose to an already beaten French Army. On June 22, France capitulated. With the Tientsin Anglo-Chinese College and the London Missionary Society unit based in the French concession at Tientsin, the Japanese were bound by the terms of the Axis Treaty of 1940 to shut down the French enclave, whch was, after all, an extension of the beaten, occupied nation in Europe.

With Britain's own future uncertain at home, and the situations collapsing rapidly in China, Eric and Florence decided in August to keep their regular missionary furlough schedule and return to duty. Theirs was a small steamer, part of a convoy of fifty vessels. The ships sailed in five parallel columns, and just off the Irish coast, their transport was hit by a torpedo. Eric must have been destined to return to China, for the torpedo failed to explode. The convoy went into its zig-zag defensive procedures, and later another ship was hit and sunk. They spent the night on deck in life jackets, and perhaps that had something to do with the bad cough that little 'Tricia,' as her father called Patricia, developed on that voyage.

For the next three days, the ships sailed at high speed using tactics to evade the enemy. Eric and Florence wondered if they had done the right thing bringing the children into this situation. The ship was in a continuous state of emergency, so that on Sunday the captain could not leave the bridge, and Eric was asked to conduct the service. He inquired if anyone minded that he had only "a sports jacket and flannels," an ironic question coming from a rural missionary who went about Chinese villages in a quilted peasant field coat. Due to the circumstances, of course, the passengers were not so concerned with a proper dress code, and he gave a service of thanksgiving. By the time they reached Nova Scotia, a total of five ships, all cargo hulls, had been sunk from the original convoy of fifty. Later, they would learn that the German government had declared the waters around Britain to be a "sphere of intensive operations" for the U-boat wolf-packs just two days after their convoy had passed out of that zone.

Patricia and Heather came down with German measles just as the ship was to dock. They passed quarantine inspection on the grounds that they had only 200 miles to go, but then there was nowhere to stay because the only hotels were full. So they went back to the ship to sleep, only to find that the bedding had been stripped.

Eric and Florence had the time to reconsider going on to China because of the World War situation, but there really was no doubt concerning the decision that they had made about the future. "I loaded all the heavy luggage for Vancouver," reported Eric, "and a few pieces for Toronto." Always, the call to China! The homeland might soon be invaded across the Channel. The China they knew was already occupied, and the enclave from which they ministered by treaty privilege was being closed out. But the missionary service had issued a call to battle that Eric and Florence could not refuse.

Upon their arrival in Toronto, where the Liddells spent ten days with the Mackenzies, they found the men of Canada signing up to fight the

Germans, for the Canadians followed Britain into both world wars long before America. Even some American volunteers served in the Canadian Armed Services before the U.S. Congress declared war. The family reunion passed quickly, and Eric, Florence, and the girls took the long train ride again to Vancouver. On the steamer, crossing the Pacific westward, there were no Japanese submarines firing torpedoes, but there was much talk about the ominous intentions of the Japanese navy. No one was too worried though, for the U.S. Navy Base at Pearl Harbor was known to be impregnable to anything the Japanese could muster.

They arrived at Tientsin the last week of October 1940. Japanese occupation forces just outside the gate of the French enclave were openly hostile. Down at Siaochang, the mission station had been made into a walled fort, and infantry battles were within hearing of the station all the time. There was a rumor that the Japanese district commander wanted the missionaries out of Siaochang because they inhibited his control of the Chinese populace. And the news that Eric received from Scotland was just as grim: the German Luftwaffe had unleashed a savage bomber campaign against the industrial heartland of England. Rob and Ernest were in the thick of it. Mother and Jenny were safe in Edinburgh, out of bomber range, at least, but Scotland was becoming one big military base.

Thirty-four years before, when Eric was a little boy at Siaochang, he had cried about the plight of the lost sheep in the hymn, "There Were Ninety-and-Nine that Safely Lay," but he had told his mother that he was only laughing so they would not stop singing the hymn. In the final weeks of 1940, all through the Hopei Province, nearly all the sheep had strayed from the safety of the folds, and there was little laughter among those who remained. But no one was laughing very much at home in Britain, either; Prime Minister Winston Churchill was calling upon even the children and the elderly to fight the German invaders from behind every building, every hedgerow, every wall. In such a situation, Eric and Florence did not consider it heroic to stay in China to be missionaries. It was simply what God had called them to do, as He had called both of their parents before them.

*W*hen the Japanese closed down the mission at Siaochang in February 1940, Miss Annie Buchan was faced with a decision. Some of the staff went over to Tsian, some to the big Union Hospital at Peking, and some were allowed to stay right at the Mackenzie Memorial Hospital in Tientsin. Thus, when Miss Annie "secured a place," as she put it, right near the Tientsin Anglo Chinese College, she once again was working nearby when Eric and Florence returned from Canada.

In the fall of 1940, Eric gave some depressing reports on how the Japanese were transforming Siaochang into an armed military camp. Men from the district were pressed into service and made to improve the road and build walls. Yet late in November, he became lyrical over a Christian wedding that he performed in another rural village, the bridegroom being a Chinese convert from the Siaochang station.

"This Friday was a day of preparation," he reported. "I wanted to gather the people together for worship that night, but the enemy had moved up and were stationed at a village less than three miles away. People were afraid to come out. However, we had evening prayers with all who were there.

Eric went on to tell how the bridegroom arrived the next day in elegant wedding garb and began the round of services and dinners. "And so," continued Eric, "the world goes on as if all were calm and quiet. The heavier guns could be heard that evening only a mile away. . . . But in Huo Chu we just met together for a service of prayer, praise and thanks." And as he was leaving this wedding, he was mistaken for a patrol of the Eighth Route Army and fired upon. He didn't dwell on his brush with death, however; he was happy over a new section of villages he was going to visit soon.

The man who was too old for the Royal Air Force was bicycling all about the district. He reported how the Japanese troops were desecrating ancient burial grounds, seizing land, and shaking people down for money and food. Christmas of 1940 found rumors circulating everywhere that the British, French, and Americans would soon be made to leave, or perhaps they would be interned. There was tremendous tension in the enclaves at Tientsin, but the British missionaries were especially aware of the furies over the skies of their home country as the RAF locked in battle with the Luftwaffe. For once, the sad news describing fighting and casualties was worse in the mails coming in to China from Britain than the reverse.

After the turn of the year, Eric rode his bicycle to villages to the south and west of Tientsin three or four days a week. It was dangerous, not just because of the Japanese units, but because of bad roads, starving Chinese civilians who would rob to stay alive, and occasionally undisciplined Chinese Army troops. In February, he plunged into work on his *Manual of Christian Discipleship,* which developed his 1937 effort into a complete Bible study course with readings and historical examples. Florence took a great interest in his work and, after she had left China, it would make them feel closer to each other as he continued his research and writings and wrote to her about how it was going.

Florence could not have been very happy in early March, 1941, for she discovered she was pregnant, and it was now a certainty that British subjects would be interned. Eric had about one month to spend with her and the girls, as field work in the district was becoming impossible. In early April, after much prayer and discussion, Florence agreed with Eric that the best thing to do was for her to return to Canada with the girls. Who knows, maybe after the baby was born and strong enough to travel, she would come back out to China with three children. Things always had worked out for the Mackenzies and the Liddells before, no matter how turbulent the political scene might be!

So in May, Florence, Patricia, and Heather sailed away for the last time. Their departure coincided with the removal of many other British, French, Dutch, and American overseas families; the ships were loaded with them as they came out of China, French Indochina, Malaya, the Philippines, and smaller military outposts and diplomatic enclaves. And Florence was not uniquely naive, for many an American wife thought she would be taking her children back in a few months to join their father in the Orient, after this business was taken care of about the Japanese flexing their military muscle.

Miss Annie Buchan correctly saw the end coming for the mission hospital presence in Tientsin and began harassing the Japanese district office for permission to transfer to the Peking Union Memorial Hospital. It was the premier medical facility in that part of the world, and, at first, her request was denied. Miss Annie is very short, very patient, and very persistent; after a week of seeing the "Siaochang Matron" in his office at Tientsin, the commander gave up and let her go to Peking, with the proviso that she must not return. Her work for the next several months in Peking would provide interesting material for a great book about Christian medical missionary service.

When Florence left for Canada, Eric moved in with the Reverend A.P. Cullen and shared his flat until January of 1942. The Reverend Cullen spent more time with Eric during his forty-three years than any other human being. He was Eric's professor of science at Eltham College until joining the staff at the TACC in 1918. He was Eric's teaching colleague at the TACC when Eric came out to China in 1925. Now they were flatmates, and soon they would be fellow internees.

"The most noteworthy feature in Eric's life," said Professor Cullen in 1945, "was the regular and rapid progress of his spiritual development. In recent years he laid much emphasis on the teaching in the Sermon on the Mount, which, he was convinced, embodied a really practical way of living, indeed the only practical way of living for a Christian. . . . To him the supreme thing about God was God's love, even as love is the supreme necessity for a truly Christian life. Another of his favorite passages was the thirteenth chapter of First Corinthians."

Eric now had lots of time to work on his *Manual,* and his ministry was increasingly limited to prayer meetings and services among the missionary and foreign community right in Tientsin. In September came the cablegram from Canada: Florence had safely delivered a girl to be called Maureen. He returned a simple answer. "Wonderful news. Love, Eric."

In Japan, there was a struggle between the militants and the moderates in Emperor Hirohito's government, and the militants won out. Powerful naval forces put to sea; if the Germans could breach the vaunted Maginot Line following years of operating within a military construction moratorium, who knew what the Imperial Fleet might accomplish at Pearl Harbor? And on December 7, 1941, several thousand men paid the ultimate price of soldiers and sailors in service to a political democracy, when the forces of evil are allowed to make the first move. Several young naval officers at Pearl Harbor were 1941 Annapolis graduates whose baccalaureate sermon had been delivered by the Reverend Peter Marshall, who had wanted to follow Eric's missionary career.

Eric Liddell hated war, even if a bit of marching "smartened up" his boys a bit. But the Apostle Paul had written to the Ephesians about the need to struggle against evil. "Put on the whole armour of God, that ye may be able to stand against the wiles of the devil. For ye wrestle not against flesh and blood, but against principalities, against powers, against the rulers of the darkness of this world, against spiritual wickedness in high places" (6:11, 12). On December 8, the Japanese commander ordered the French concession at Tientsin closed.

Eric now moved in with the family of a British Methodist missionary, the Reverend D. Howard Smith, who had a home in the British enclave. The Reverend Smith was later to be interned with Eric, and he wrote about those final hectic months in Tientsin, when the Japanese had put an electrified fence around the British enclave and limited public gatherings to no more than ten people.

Church services, under such a rule, were impossible, and so Eric did what he liked best—holding prayer meetings with individuals and small groups within the enclave. He became the ideal house guest. The Smith children were thrilled to have the famous athlete living with them. He taught them tennis and cricket. He got up early and stood in the long lines where the rationed food was issued. When the spring dust storms blanketed the Smith house with coats of the choking tan powder, Eric got up at four A.M. and washed all the horizontal surfaces. He took long walks with Professor A.P. Cullen, and he kept working on his *Manual*.

In August 1942, Eric received an offer to take up a rural pastorate ("sphere" it was called) in western Canada. He wrote to Florence that perhaps they should take it after the war; he knew it would be hard work, but that is what God called them to do. He also included a progress report on his *Manual*, for he knew she maintained interest in this aspect of his work. In September, he also investigated the idea of resuming his rural missionary beat in the Hopei Province with the Japanese authorities.

In the fall, internment was certain. The Allies were concerned that Chiang Kai-shek might be lured into a separate peace with the Japanese, since he wanted to fight the Chinese Communist forces, and the Japanese were posing as liberators of Asia from the Western white man. So all historical treaty concessions were renounced. This meant that Eric and the missionaries in the British compound were now living in occupied China, which was formally at war against Germany, and therefore against Japan through the Axis Treaty.

In October, Eric read several novels about World War I and the social protests that followed it. He commented upon the biography of a famous missionary who died young, "one of those men whose work is finished at 36, but who, by that time, are ready to join the Choir Invisible." His *Manual for Christian Discipleship* was approaching completion, and he credited others with writing most of the contents. Rigorous analysis later showed the arrangements of the scriptural ideas with human issues to be vintage Eric Liddell. One page was actually an example of Eric's daily routine that was known to his family and friends on both sides of the globe. It was evidently the source of his serenity:

Suggested Questions Which You Might Find
Helpful For Your Daily Morning Quiet.

1. Have I surrendered this new day to God, and will I seek and obey the guidance of the Holy Spirit throughout its hours?
2. What have I specially to thank God for this morning?
3. Is there any sin in my life for which I should seek Christ's forgiveness and cleansing? Is there any apology or restitution to make?
4. For whom does God want me to pray this morning?
5. What bearing does this morning's Bible passage have on my life, and what does He want me to do about it?
6. What does God want me to do today and how does He want me to do it?

Eric functioned as "correspondent," a kind of elected representative or spokesperson, for the British Residents' Committee before the Japanese district commander. He called a meeting on March 12, 1943, and gave the news they all knew had been coming. British, American, and other non-Oriental nationals were to be interned at Weihsien, down in the Shantung Province. The location was actually an American Presbyterian Mission, isolated a bit out in the country where the Japanese garrison could control its occupants with minimum forces, and it was to be called a "Civil Assembly Centre."

All foreigners to be interned from Tientsin and the surrounding area would be sent out on three train lifts on March 23, 28, and 30. Eric, as "correspondent," would go on the last lift. Each person could take three suitcases or trunks, and a bed with bedding materials. It was all very efficient, and the China Inland Mission newsletter carried a notice about it for their supporters in Britain. The Japanese organized the move carefully, and Eric set about to help the people who needed him. St. Paul had written about times like this.

"Thou therefore endure hardness, as a good soldier of Jesus Christ. No man that warreth entangleth himself with the affairs of this life; that he may please him who hath chosen him to be a soldier. And if a man also strive for masteries, yet he be not crowned, except he strive lawfully" (2 Timothy 2:3-5). Eric had discussed this passage many times during the campaigns among the student athletes. And now he would go as a soldier of the missionary service to a place where 1,800 people from eleven foreign countries and several faiths would live in less space than criminals were guaranteed in British and American prisons.

Eric went down on the last train to the Weihsien compound on March 30, 1943. He stayed awake most of the night for the trip. Right away, it seemed to be his job to cheer everybody up, to give reassurance in this move that was upsetting to families with children. He did not feel sorry for himself about the fact that his own children were halfway around the world.

The American Presbyterian Missions Board had built a facility about two miles outside of Weihsien in the early 1900s, while the surge of evangelical interest in China was high. It served the same function in its portion of the Shantung Province that the London Missionary Society's installation at Siaochang fulfilled in the adjacent Hopei Province. The occupying Japanese forces seized the Weihsien facility the day after the attack upon Pearl Harbor.

Inflamed with anti-American fervor, Japanese military personnel had damaged the furniture and some of the structures at Weihsien. Then, in a more sober moment, they recognized that the facility would be a useful location for interning the European and American non-combatants. So a small detachment of security troops took the best building and living quarters, and they put an electrified, barbed wire fence around the remainder, with searchlights at the guard towers on the corners. Broken furniture was still strewn all about as the internees arrived late in March 1943. When the movement instructions were being given out at Tientsin, Chefoo, and the other sources of internees, the Japanese did not point out that all the cooking utensils and dishes had been destroyed or stolen by their security force.

In 1943 the compound filled to its complement of 1,800 internees, living in a total space of 150 square feet of living space and 18 square feet of sleeping area for each person. But even this computation is deceptive, for the largest building was the hospital, a four-story structure that was long on medical missionary staff but critically short on drugs, medications, and expendable supplies of all kinds. The fourth floor, once a spacious residential facility for the medical missionary staff, became a crowded dormitory for family units as the internees poured in.

Eric's first living assignment was a room shared with two other missionary pastors. Each one had a space that measured nine by thirteen feet, and they occupied this area for five months. In another building, married couples with one or more children occupied a room of the same size. Eventually, the children above the age of puberty were placed in separate dorms for boys or for girls, but some of the parents had concerns about the supervision of their youngsters in this situation. Eric became one of the people who worked with this difficult problem of what to do with the older children. Memoirs from missionary internee centers in Hong Kong, Manila, and other Japanese occupied regions suggest that the problem was common to them all, and that the solutions often were provided by missionary personalities like Eric Liddell, who could get the long days filled with sports, academics, and prayer groups.

The Japanese camp commander exercised his authority through a civil affairs liaison officer and a military police commander who was in direct authority over the guards. Japanese military personnel conducted two roll calls daily to insure that no escapes occurred. Otherwise, social contact between Japanese soldiers and the internees was minimal. Escapes and disciplinary problems were discouraged by the camp's own management committee, because these things could lead to reprisals. In addition to the Discipline Committee, the internees operated departments of Education, Entertainment, and Athletics. Since the missionary presence in China was loaded with teachers, nurses, and doctors, plus ministers who were skilled teachers and youth counselors, the children at Weihsien, as well as at other camps, often received an exemplary education.

There was the Employment Committee, which supervised and allocated the mandatory three hours of daily labor that all able-bodied internees were required to donate. This rule was self-imposed. The Engineering and Repairs Committee organized a campaign to rebuild the damaged furniture and facilities that greeted the arriving interness in March of 1943. The missionaries in China always had been accustomed to doing a lot with a little, and in record time they produced a remarkably civilized, if crowded, living compound.

The Finance Committee worked out an arrangement with the Swiss Red Cross representative to create a small account for those internees who had an outside source of income. They even were able to operate a small canteen store at Weihsien, and arrangements were made to provide a little spending money and some amenities for those who were completely destitute of income. The General Affairs Committee wrestled with coordinating the activities of all the other committees, and with articulating camp policy under the rules of the Japanese commander and the International Red Cross.

The Quarters and Accommodation Committee had the impossible job of trying to provide living space that did not exist, and to distribute what there was among a mixed situation of families, single adults, children without families, and a variety of religious groups that had specific dogmas about living arrangements. The fact that eleven nationalities and five languages existed among the internees complicated things a bit, too. The Supplies Committee did its best to allocate, and, while there would be post-war accusations that this or that person exploited some situation, sober reconsideration suggests that these accusations are more in the category of sour grapes. In reality, the behavior of the internees was exemplary, given the extremely difficult circumstances.

In April, an English language newspaper became available to Weihsien; however, the news was censored. The internees followed the progress of the war by reading reports of how the Imperial Forces had just fought magnificently at such-and-such a location, following which a strategic reassignment of troops was being made to somewhere nearer Japan! Other incoming news was provided by Red Cross messages that started out with a one-hundred word limit, but were later limited to twenty-five words.

It is not certain how much Eric knew about the sad news within his own family during his internment at Weihsien. Lieutenant Ernest Liddell suffered a severe cranial injury resulting from an accident during artillery operations. As a result, he was able later on to hold his position with an Edinburgh bank after the war, and he had a family; but he was always subject to severe headaches and periods when he could not function well. Eric's mother became terminally ill and, although she knew that the Battle of Britain turned out favorably, much of Eric's story was kept from her.

When Eric had been turned down for service as a pilot by the RAF, another Olympic champion was signed up as a pilot by the U.S. Marine Corps. This was Charley Paddock, who had been an artillery lieutenant in the U.S. Army during World War I and was exempt from further service both as a veteran of the previous war, and because of age. Charley had nosed out Eric for the silver medal in the 200-meter race in Paris in 1924, had gone on to inspire young Jesse Owens to train for championship athletics, and had pursued a desultory career as a movie actor. In April of 1943, while Eric was just setting up his routine as a teacher and a coach of sports, Charley Paddock was killed in Alaska when his plane crashed.

Eric's assignment for the first five months at Weihsien was to teach secondary mathematics for one half of each day, and athletics of all kinds during the other half of the day. He conducted Protestant services, performed social assistance in several forms, served on the official Discipline Committee, and was the overall coordinator of camp sporting events. The missionaries decided from the outset that the internment would be turned from a tribulation into an opportunity, which, after all, was the kind of theological premise that had brought them to China in the first place.

There was class all day for the children, and a wide variety of adult education classes which could be attended on a voluntary basis. Eric broadened his instruction in mathematics into the teaching of science and chemistry to a few advanced secondary students. He made up for the lack of scientific equipment by all sorts of imaginative means. For one girl, he drew a whole notebook full of diagrams, showing the equipment she would have used in secondary chemistry. She was able to enroll after the war directly into an Australian university. Several more students moved directly into British and American universities without further preparatory study.

The internees at Weihsien ate at long wooden tables in the camp dining hall. They were organized administratively into three groups, based on the city from which they were interned—Tsingtao, Tientsin, and Peking. Each group had its own dining hall staff, and each person provided his or her own dishes and cutlery. It was possible, until close to the end of the war, to augment the food with purchases from the canteen. Occasionally available were such things as peanuts, eggs, candy, honey, fruit, toothpaste, and a few clothing items of Chinese manufacture. The Red Cross in northern China was not able to provide food or clothing parcels to internees, but there were a few sympathetic Japanese and non-interned Europeans who sent food and items of personal utility to Weihsien.

The main thing that kept the Weihsien community bound together was the social program of sports, plays, musical productions, and lectures. The missionaries of all the different faiths cooperated well, so that while there were religious programs available to believers of all persuasions, no one was ever forced by the circumstances of internment to participate in religious practices that opposed their personal beliefs.

The entire program at Weihsien turned towards an emphasis on youth because of an administrative decision by the Japanese forces in northeast China. On August 27, 1943, the city of Chefoo was seized, and the school operated there by the missionaries for their own children was taken over for military use. Some of the parents of the students enrolled in 1943 were informed that the Japanese would leave the school intact. Chefoo had been selected by the China Inland Mission for the site of a school and administrative center back in the 1870s because of its political stability and its open access to foreign travel and customs. Jenny had attended this school. Now, the entire student population was to be interned. Some of the parents were already interned in different locations, and some could not be located at all. Yet out of these children of the Chefoo School would come some remarkable alumni, several of whom would continue the traditions of the missionary service into another era.

In the summer of 1943, Madame Chiang Kai-shek was extremely active in recruiting American and British support for her husband's Kuomintang regime. While the appeal, of course, was to enlist allies in the common cause of expelling the Japanese invaders, it would later become clear that she sought allies for the struggle against Mao Tse-tung and the Chinese Communists. Out of the effort would grow the "China lobby," and the unsupportable notion that Chiang Kai-shek could have been kept in power in China after 1950, if only the State Department and contentious General Joseph Stilwell had been made to see the light in time. But for Eric and his family, it meant that highly flattering reports about the work of the British and American missionaries in China were now furnished to patriotic audiences in their homelands, and pressure was put on the Japanese government to treat them in a humane manner.

Eric obtained an assignment to the Weihsien Civil Affairs officer as translator, which should put to rest any speculation about his linguistic abilities. He had lived for twelve years, minus time as a rural missionary, at the French enclave in Tientsin. His Chinese was good enough for the college educated city folk and for the rural people as well. He had Japanese friends among the evangelical community for years, and members of the governing committees at Weihsien learned some functional Japanese in a hurry. Consequently, Eric was in a perfect position to know what was going on about the camp. He soon demonstrated an amazing capacity to explain the progress of the war, even when the censored English language newspaper blocked out entire events which showed that the Axis powers were losing.

Two Chinese internees at Weihsien had escaped in the first days. After that, there never were any more escapes, which is fortunate, since Japanese officers often beheaded selected victims or camp leaders in reprisal for escapes by civilians as well as military prisoners from their camps. But these two escapees had fled far to the south, linked up with Chinese Nationalist forces, and joined an information-passing apparatus. They returned to a secret location in the Shantung Province, and from their clandestine radio station received reports on the real location and extent of Allied military operations. Consequently, Eric always knew, right up until the end, the progress of the war, but he did not reveal his source for security reasons.

On July 12, 1943, Miss Annie Buchan arrived at Weihsien. "On arrival," she reported, ". . . I was faced with a mass of faces peering through the bars of a big iron gate. The internees were terribly thin and thinly clad: some were in ragged and tattered fur coats which well-to-do ladies had taken into camp with them. . . . A number of my missionary colleagues were at Weihsien, so I was among friends . . . Eric Liddell was an inspiration, and he had an enthusiastic team of willing workers with ideas that appealed to the young people."

And why was Miss Annie, who had harrassed the Japanese authorities into assigning her to the Union Hospital at Peking, suddenly interned at Weihsien?

It seems that Miss Annie had been perfectly willing to care equally for the sick, wounded, and injured of all persuasions at Peking. But even today, over forty years and still another China war later, she remembers becoming involved in a number of escapades, on the margins of the Japanese rules, to provide care and food for people who needed it. Once, she sent a wounded Chinese officer out with the mortuary detail, tagged with a death certificate, after learning that the Japanese planned to kill him in his hospital bed. It is very possible that the Japanese authorities decided she was a thorn in their flesh. At any rate, she was told that she would be interned at Weihsien.

"I showed them the card I had received from their authorities, which stated that because I had been humane I would be exempt from camp. Where was I going, and why?"

"Britain not humane," answered the Japanese administrator. "We, Japanese, humane."

"Later," continued Miss Annie, "I learned that the reason was because two men had escaped from Weihsien (Eric Liddell's intelligence network!) and I was a reprisal. These two men were the only escapees in the three-and-a-half years of internment; they joined a Chinese group of guerrillas, and were with them when the war ended." Thus were the affairs of Eric and Miss Annie intertwined. On the train to Weihsien, Miss Annie read from her Bible, and the message she got from the many passages she read was: "My presence shall go with thee. Be strong and of good courage. Fear not, nor be afraid of them." When she arrived, the Japanese took her Bible; she prayed, and later a Japanese officer returned it.

On August 30, 1943, the children from the Chefoo School were brought down river by boat and interned together. They were added to the more than 500 children already in the camp, about half without parents and the rest unsure if their parents were even alive. Miss Annie set to work getting the hospital in shape, although she is quick to say that other nurses who arrived before her were already doing a top job with limited resources. One measure of the excellence of the overall medical program in the Weihsien camp is that there was never an epidemic of any kind among the children.

The arrival of the Chefoo children resulted in the final change in Eric's ministry. He was moved to become the supervisor of the younger children's dormitory. These children became the final, temporary replacement in his life for Pat, Heather, and Maureen in Canada. He conducted the roll call, checked them for health needs, taught them math and science, enrolled them in Sunday School and Bible study, and, in general, was "Uncle Eric" to them all. One day each week he spent entirely with the children to give the other teachers a break.

Eric's work load now was excessive. To add to that stress on his body, the food rations diminished as Japan was losing the war. And, finally, an arterial deterioration was beginning in his brain, as yet undiscovered. Yet in 1944, he was the absolute, unquestioned moral sparkplug of the Weihsien camp.

Eric organized athletic meets and thrilled everyone by running exhibition races himself. He steadfastly refused to have the matches on Sunday, but, once when the children fought during a Sunday game they had organized, he relented to the extent of becoming the referee for the Sunday athletics events. A few times he also violated his own personal rule and told stories about the Olympic Games, about his wild leap to the deck of a steamer at Port Arthur. He taught the children to play basketball, soccer, rounders, even American baseball. In his Sunday school class, he taught them his favorite hymn:

> Be still, my soul, the Lord is on thy side;
> Bear patiently the cross of grief or pain;
> Leave to thy God to order and provide;
> In every change He faithful will remain.
> Be still, my soul, thy best, thy heavenly Friend
> Through thorny ways leads to a joyful end.

And he often based his lessons upon 1 Corinthians 13 and Matthew 5.

When Margery Brameld, Miss Annie's long-time friend and colleague in the missionary service, died on February 19, 1944, Eric offered a moving and prophetic eulogy. "God gives gifts from many friendships. There was Margery's friendship with Annie. It is difficult to know what makes friendships, for their characters were entirely different. Theirs, however, was a beautiful friendship and, in our Mission in years to come, we shall speak of it as of the friendship of David and Jonathan." And Eric spent long night hours at the deathbed of two patients on Miss Annie's ward in the hospital—the daughter of a widow in the camp and a Roman Catholic nun. Eric fixed up some shelves in the apartment of a Russian prostitute in the camp, and she reported that he was the only man of her acquaintance who had ever done her a favor and refused her services as payment.

At Christmas 1944, Professor A.P. Cullen and Miss Annie Buchan were talking about their years in the China missionary service. He gave her a Christmas card with a message: "God gave us memory that we might have roses in December." Dozens of children at Weihsien would remember Uncle Eric, and many would be glad that he, and not the Japanese military police guards, were in charge of the discipline at the camp. Eric handled the punishment of a youth who was caught climbing the trees near the guard towers, where there were electric search lights and machine guns. Eric also consoled the mother of another child who had been electrocuted while touching the wires that brought power to those same searchlights.

As late as December 1944, Eric still maintained his supremely cheerful, serene disposition. He was active in the Christmas pageant. The Salvation Army Band had brought their instruments to the camp and was a great favorite. Music, prayer, counseling, self-produced plays—these were the things that Eric and the missionary leaders used to bring people through their experience of internment. Eric's smile, his twinkling blue eyes, his easy catalog of blessings—all these things are still remembered many years later by the people who were there. He could always laugh at himself in a charming, natural way, such as the continuing jokes about the outrageous shirt he often wore: a floral pattern made from Florence's curtains that once hung in the family home at Tientsin. The shirt looked like a Hawaiian model, and the internees laughed over the tale of Eric's departure for a clergy meeting in 1932, dressed like Duke Kahanamoku.

But just after Christmas 1944, Eric's body was wearing out. He knew something was wrong; they told him in the hospital that it was fatigue, malnourishment, a passing bout of influenza. But he could not see clearly out of one eye, and his leg had a curious way of folding up underneath him. He prayed and studied his Bible. "I press toward the mark for the prize of the high calling of God in Christ Jesus" (Philippians 3:14). He confided only to Miss Annie Buchan that there was something seriously wrong with him inside his head.

In Edinburgh, Eric's mother was too ill to know even the little bits of news that came in the twenty-five word Red Cross messages to Florence, relayed in letters to Scotland. And that little country had taken tens of thousands of American boys into their homes and their hearts, boys who would soon join in on the greatest seaborne invasion of all history along the Normandy beaches. In hundreds of these temporary homes where American boys found love in Scotland, their own son had already died in north Africa, France, or out in the Pacific. In Scotland, and out at Weihsien, the call was the same: "Fight the good fight of faith, lay hold on eternal life, whereunto thou art called, and hast professed a good profession before many witnesses" (Timothy 1:12).

Sports writers had always said that Eric was slow coming off the block. His defenders in later years attributed this quality to the idea that he was so moral, so ethical in all things, that he feared to get an advantage of any kind over the other runners. But coming into the stretch, he was formidable. When "his heid went back," they said in Scotland, he could not be beaten. But now it was a terrible physical disorder inside his head that would take him to the tape for the last time. God's joyful runner was still smiling, but he was coming up on the tape at high speed.

One of the burdens of being a person who lives to console others is that the sympathetic listener can be perceived as one who never has any troubles to bear. But Eric did not consider the carrying of other peoples' troubles a burden; rather it was a blessing.

The food supply to the camp dwindled, and the effects of malnutrition and fatigue took its toll on Eric. Furthermore, the tumor on Eric's brain was growing, and sometimes the healer needs healing. Eric confided only in Miss Annie Buchan, seeking consolation not for himself, but for his family.

"My big worry, Annie," he said, "is that I didn't give Flo enough of my time."

With that statement Eric had in mind the weeks he had spent apart from her and the babies, beginning in the fall of 1937. And, of course, there was the decision to send Florence and the girls home to Canada in May of 1941. Miss Annie, of course, consoled Eric by reminding him of the obvious: Flo and the girls were safe in Canada; the absences were caused by work in God's service, and Florence was a daughter of the China missionary service.

"But that's not all of it, Annie," he said. "I can't see any future. Everything looks blank."

For the man whose personal faith was cited by others as the model, the standard, this statement was totally uncharacteristic. But Miss Annie was a missionary nurse, and she knew that there are medical syndromes which alter the outlook of even the most devout believer. She considered the possibility that he was suffering from a clinical depression due to the circumstances at the camp. No one at that time had any idea that Eric was terminally ill. Eric was not renouncing his faith with that statement, not condemning God; he was simply expressing a rare commodity in his otherwise God-controlled life—the human emotion called regret.

"It wasn't like Eric," said Miss Annie much later. "He was always so full of hope. What he called 'not being able to see the future' was probably the tumor at work. . . ."

In the late fall of 1944, Eric was spending more time looking at his photographs of Florence and the girls. Of course, when they parted in 1941, Eric had no indication that he thought he was telling his family goodbye forever. "Those who love God never meet for the last time" was the motto of the gentle knights. And Florence! "It just never crossed my mind for a minute," she said years later. "I thought it would be one or two years. Even right at the end, it never crossed my mind that anything could happen to Eric."

Florence did not live in Scotland during those years when Eric's track fans believed he could not be beaten when "his heid went back." Eric never once in his life bragged of invincibility, not on the track, not at rugby, and certainly not in the hazardous backlands of China. It was just that his faith, his serenity, his deep joy in every act of service, made people assume he would endure. "I don't know how I could have been so naive," Florence said long afterwards.

Several internees had not even known that he had a family, for he always started conversations with questions about the well-being of the other person's family.

"There were other persons in the same position," one of the survivors later reported, "who went round moaning that they had not seen their wives. But Eric was so busy cheering other people up that he kept his own miseries and problems very much to himself. . . . He was a very private person. I remember being quite surprised at finding out how close he and Flo actually were."

For all but a very few, however, Eric remained the healer. It was long after the liberation that internees found out some of the things he had done. As a member of the Camp Disciplinary Committee he would become aware of cases in which someone had shirked the job of carrying buckets of coal for the older and physically incapacitated internees. This was the same Eric who, as Captain of the Rugby XV at Eltham, could not yell at the unenthusiastic player. He responded to the non-carrying of coal by carrying it himself! Well, no one ever said that Eric was the world's best disciplinarian, but it is interesting to note how he did agree to referee the youngsters' games on Sunday, an action that came very close to his notion of violating the Fourth Commandment, but only he could handle the games without acrimonious disputes arising among the players.

In January 1945, the Japanese occupation forces siphoned off the rations for most of the internment and prison camps to such a degree that malnutrition led to starvation in many cases. The International Red Cross in northeast China up to that time had not been sending in food parcels, but on January 31, 1945, a special Red Cross shipment of basic foodstuffs arrived at Weihsien. Pressure by the Allies and the Red Cross on the Japanese government resulted in some improvement during the ensuing weeks, but then reverted almost completely in the final eight weeks before Japan's surrender.

By the time the rations were improving in late January, Eric was in the camp hospital. The diagnosis, as he reported it to a medical missionary friend, was a nervous breakdown. But people like Eric did not have nervous breakdowns, not in the way the word was used in those days, for there was an implication that the person somehow could not employ self-control to his or her own condition. And Eric was known among the missionary community for his serenity and composure. Others who knew a little of his illness thought he might be suffering from influenza, as there was an epidemic in January; another believable explanation was the combined effects of malnutrition and the fifteen to eighteen-hour-a-day list of tasks Eric had assigned himself. But Eric was becoming increasingly aware of something seriously wrong. There was partial paralysis of his legs, his one eye drooped off oddly, and he had headaches so severe only he and God will ever know the degree of suffering he endured.

A friend, catching the edges of this situation, asked him in the hospital if there were any improvement in the trouble inside his head. And neither Eric nor the friend took the question for a pun about the quality of his thinking.

"To answer that question," Eric replied, "I'd need to know what was going on inside my head."

Meanwhile, decisions were being made that determined the outcome of the war. General Joe Stilwell, that great American expert on China, was playing out his time as Commander of the China theater. "Vinegar Joe" had once been President of the Union Language School in Peking when Miss Annie Buchan attended it as a student in 1925. Obsessed with the notion that Generalissimo Chiang Kai-shek's concern about the Red Army of Mao Tse-tung was mere warlordism, Stilwell used his direct access to U.S. Army Chief of Staff George C. Marshall time and again to paint a picture that Chiang Kai-shek was merely biding his time, letting others take the casualties, and doing nothing to prosecute the war against the Japanese Army.

While General Stilwell was intellectually brilliant and eminently knowledgeable about Chinese history and language, he repeatedly offended British, French, Chinese, and even American leaders of the other armed forces and agencies. In February, General Marshall recalled General Stilwell and replaced him with the diplomatic and intellectual Lt. General Albert C. Wedemeyer.

U.S. and British forces in China were light and mostly concentrated in the south. But at the same time that Lt. General Wedemeyer took over, the hammer was falling on island after island in the Pacific, closing in on the Japanese mainland. One of these islands, Iwo Jima, would be symbolic of what was to come, should it be necessary to invade the mainland. On February 19, the invasion of Iwo Jima began.

Lt. General Wedemeyer began planning ways to use his considerable air transport capability. The Chinese Nationalist Army had assault forces and Wedemeyer began ferrying troops to strengthen the Nationalist effort in northern China, where the Chinese Red Army was strongest in opposing the Japanese. Liberation of prison camps and internee centers was a humanitarian task included in the plans, but a task of relatively low priority. The goal was to defeat the Japanese with Nationalist China's troops so that the Red Army would not seize power quickly as the Japanese forces surrendered.

Miss Annie Buchan got most of her news about daily life at the Weihsien camp from Eric Liddell. He often was at the hospital to visit her patients, and she seldom was allowed to be anywhere else. When Eric sought to be admitted during the mid-January influenza epidemic, she knew he was desperately sick, for he would not give in to illness. There was no available space. "I just went straight on to the head doctor," she said, "and told him that Eric would have to be admitted.

Eric would not have been there wanting to be let in unless he were terribly sick."

The camp doctors discussed Eric's symptoms—the malfunctioning leg, the slurred speech, the violent headaches, dizziness, and the uncharacteristic depression. The possibility of a brain tumor was mentioned. There was little to be done in those days except to treat the symptoms, whether in Weihsien or at the Edinburgh University Hospital. The program of rest and better diet helped somewhat, and the influenza dissipated. But the most telling symptoms—the leg that did not function right and the headaches—did not abate.

After three weeks in the hospital, Eric rallied. A young couple came to see him, and he counseled them about their upcoming marriage. He even discussed social details, and he obviously intended to be part of future events. In February 11 he suffered what was called a slight stroke, which was probably the partial rupture of a cranial artery. His leg remained paralyzed thereafter, although only a few people knew how badly.

It was in this condition that he climbed four flights of steps to visit a missionary couple quartered above the hospital. A nurse had to help him all the way, and he was completely exhausted from the ordeal. The couple was shocked at Eric's physical condition. They noticed his slow speech, his haggard look. They invited him to come back a couple of days later for tea, thinking that some good food would put strength back in him. He accepted the invitation to return.

On Sunday, February 18, Eric attended services and spent some time looking at his photographs of the family. He visited with patients on the wards at the hospital and thought about writing his next Red Cross message to Florence. But why didn't food make him stronger? Why was rest not stopping the dizziness and headaches? Why did exercise not clear up the muscular soreness in his right leg? And despite Eric's own jokes about his limited medical knowledge when he acted as superintendent at the Siaochang Hospital during Rob's furlough, it is difficult to believe he did not know he had a brain tumor.

A cold weather period was moving in, and the camp Social Committee set up indoor entertainments. The Salvation Army Band had brought their instruments with them when they were interned. Each Sunday morning while Eric was in the hospital, they gave a concert; now, they gave an evening performance as well. Especially dear to him was the tune *Finlandia,* to which the words of the hymn "Be still my soul, the Lord is on thy side" went through his head as the muted brass instruments played.

It is difficult to understand the actions of other internees on Monday and Tuesday. Eric had been officially released from the hospital, was seen walking slowly about, and visited cheerfully with several people. Yet he did not teach his science classes, did not conduct roll call for his school children, and no one seems to have asked what he was doing. One may only hypothesize that Eric was so characteristically interested in others before himself, and so apparently indestructible in the way people perceived him, that no one asked the obvious: "Are you getting better, or is there something seriously the matter with you?"

It was on that Monday, February 19, that the giant amphibious assault force stormed ashore at Iwo Jima. American forces were fighting bitter house-to-house combat that month against the Japanese forces in Luzon, from time to time liberating interned packets of civilians and missionaries around Manila. Eric did not have this news, but he knew, between his interpretive reading of the English language camp newspaper and his private spy network, that Allied forces had struck deeply into Germany and the Philippines.

On Tuesday, Eric's missionary friends on the fourth floor of the hospital sent him a cake, something to which he was partial all his life. There were clouds in the sky, signaling the onset of a snowfall. Eric walked about the camp, reread his old letters, and visited Miss Annie at the hospital. She brought him up to date on several patients who had asked for him. Even at the very end, he wanted to immerse his earthly being in the troubles of others. His one regret about his recent bout in the hospital had been that he could not put his own pain and uncertainty entirely in God's hands. "There is just one thing that troubles me," he had told his missionary friends in slow, halting speech. "I ought to have been able to cast it all on the Lord, and not to have broken down under it."

On Wednesday morning, it was cold and overcast. Eric had his morning prayer time, chatted with friends at breakfast, and then set to work on a letter to Florence.

21st February, 1945. Was carrying too much responsibility. Slight nervous breakdown. Am much better after month in hospital. Doctor suggests changing my work. Giving up teaching and athletics and taking up physical work like baking . . . A good change. Keep me in touch with the news. Enjoying comfort and parcels. Special love to you and the children.—Eric.

Florence would receive this letter at Toronto in May, following its tedious passage through Red Cross channels. There were several million people interned and imprisoned by both the Allies and the Axis powers during World War II, and 1945 was the final, peak year. Thousands of volunteers in the International Red Cross handled the correspondence between these multi-national millions, crossing over hostile military lines.

Eric visited with several people and chatted with the wife of a missionary friend who worked in the hospital cafeteria at lunch time. After lunch he had a rest, then walked out on the compound. The wife of his friend came off duty and saw him, coming from the camp post office. He had just mailed his letter to Florence.

"Have you heard from Flo?" she asked him.

"Oh, yes, I've had a letter recently," replied Eric, slowly. "Flo and the girls are all well."

"I've not seen you about lately," said his friend. "You must rest up and get your strength back."

"No," replied Eric, "I must just get my walking legs again."

They parted cheerfully, and Eric went in for tea. Then he went to visit people on the hospital wards, and he seemed cheerful. The one thing that everyone noticed that seemed so uncharacteristic of Eric was the slowness of his speech and gait. But this was so easily attributed to tiredness, to recuperation from a bout with the flu! In the early evening, Eric met one of his pupils from the Sunday School class at the Tientsin Union Church where he had taught what seemed like many long years ago. The conversation was important to him, for another of his former pupils from those years was Florence Mackenzie Liddell.

Suddenly, Eric took on a choking spasm, and he was obviously in great pain. He gripped the woman's arm.

"Let me get you to the doctor," she said, deeply concerned.

"No, no, it will pass," said Eric. "I'm still getting my strength back, you know."

Half an hour or so later, he found one of his pupils from the Chefoo School who was on the ward but allowed walking privileges.

"Uncle Eric, you've come to see me!" came the greeting.

This little girl along with the others, had come to replace three little ones far away in Canada, and soon they were engaged in an animated conversation. It was Eric's last happy moment with children, for he went into a spasm of choking and could not even stand. The girl ran down the hall.

"Doctor, doctor, it's Uncle Eric," she cried. "He's terribly ill! He's choking!"

The duty nurse and doctor put Eric to bed in a private room. Miss Annie Buchan had gone off duty, and the duty nurse sent for her. She rushed immediately to his bedside.

"Eric," she said, "what do you think is the matter?"

"They haven't a clue," he replied.

The duty physician suggested to Miss Annie that she could go on to her quarters, since she had just finished a long shift.

"I'll not leave him," she said. And she stayed at his side.

But now Miss Annie saw the labored breathing and the lapses in consciousness that were the result of two more cerebral hemorrhages. She went back out into the adjacent ward, where two doctors were talking.

"Do you realize Eric is dying?" asked this diminutive woman who comforted the dying and drove Japanese officers to distraction.

"Nonsense," came the words from one of the physicians. Miss Annie went back to Eric's bedside.

He went into another convulsion, the most terrible yet. She cradled the muscular shoulders in her arms.

"Annie," he whispered, "it's complete surrender to God."

Miss Annie is not certain if he was trying to finish the sentence with, ". . . complete surrender to God's will." Either way, it was consistent with Eric's thinking, with his modes of expression, but the longer statement had been made by Eric many times before.

He lapsed into a coma, and Miss Annie ran into the ward next door to get the physicians on duty. They came, but Eric was no longer in the hands of human physicians. Miss Annie took his hand; she asked God's mercy. There were a few tears in her eyes, but she was very much in control of her emotions for Miss Annie knew precisely the mission that

God had sent her to do. Eric's mother had died; his beloved sister, Jenny, was far away in Scotland; and Florence was in Canada with the girls. Miss Annie, who braved the savagery of Chinese warlord battles, banditry, Japanese Army abuses, and, later, the Communist revolution, knew she was being called upon for a special service to Eric.

Eric's breathing slowed, and he moved only a little. In a few minutes, he gave out a final breath and then, in the strongest closing finish of his life, he broke eternity's tape. God's joyful runner had achieved his goal.

The duty physician ordered the body held for an autopsy. Next day, Miss Annie returned for this procedure, which must have torn her heart severely. But the camp authorities had to know the medical cause of Eric's death, and the reasons were not purely scientific.

"We didn't know of a certainty if the Allies were going to win," says Miss Annie. "Who knows what claim the Japanese might make later, especially if they won the war?"

On Saturday, February 24, 1945, Weihsien internment camp held the most memorable event of the entire wartime experience—Eric Liddell's funeral. Even though there was a large church, designed in happier times to accommodate the 350 or so residents of the mission and a "walk-in" congregation from the town, there were more standing outside than inside for this occasion.

As the mourners filed in, the pianist played "I Know That My Redeemer Liveth." The presiding minister was the Reverend Arnold Bryson, one of the old timers of the London Missionary Society, and he showed immediately the kind of theological awareness and toughness that characterized the thinking of the LMS pastors.

"The sudden removal of such a man in the prime of his life, and at the peak of his powers, inevitably raises questions in our hearts. Why did God take him from a world in which such men are so sorely needed today? But God makes no mistakes . . ." The Reverend Bryson speculated that perhaps God was sparing Eric from years of suffering by taking him in death at age forty-three.

"Yesterday a man said to me, 'Of all the men I have known, Eric Liddell was the one in whose character and life the spirit of Jesus Christ was pre-eminently manifested.' What was the secret of his consecrated life and far-reaching influence? Absolute surrender to God's will as revealed in Jesus Christ. His was a God-controlled life and he followed his Master and Lord with a devotion that never flagged and with an intensity of purpose that made men see both the reality and power of true religion. With St. Paul, Eric could say, 'I live, yet not I, but Christ liveth in me.' If anyone was ready for his Master's call, it was our friend, whose happy, radiant face we shall see no more on earth, but his influence will surely live on in the hearts and lives of all who knew him."

The closing hymn was "For All the Saints, Who From Their Labors Rest"; and then it was time for a procession that Eric would have liked. He had once told Florence that he wanted no long, windy eulogies, no pomp and show at his funeral. Some little distance from the big church was a cemetery where earlier missionaries lay buried, adjacent to the buiding in use by the resident Japanese garrison officers.

Cold wind, snow, and malnutrition all were forgotten. Eight colleagues of the China missionary service carried Eric's plain coffin on their shoulders to its final resting place. The honor guard, marching two-by-two, came just behind. They were Eric's pupils, the children of the Chefoo school. It was the teaching and baptizing of children that were Eric's greatest love in his ministry.

In the snow, on the side of that windswept hill in China, the Japanese guards looked down from the tower. Gathered around the gravesite, some five hundred mourners began to recite in unison the Beatitudes, so beloved of this man who taught that "meek" is submission to God's will, not weakness. The following Friday, March 3, there was a memorial service.

The Reverend A.P. Cullen presided at this service, where there was standing room only. The Reverend Cullen announced that four speakers, all long-time colleagues of Eric's, would each offer some remembrances, but first they would all sing.

"Let us sing a hymn that was for many years a favorite of Eric's," he said. "More than ten years ago Eric made a special request to have it included in a little book of hymns I was compiling for use at the Tientsin Anglo Chinese College. On the last afternoon of his life, in his weakness and having, it is clear, a premonition of his death, he wrote down a few things on some scraps of paper. Much of what he wrote is faint and illegible, but here and there it is possible to trace his words. Amongst them are the first line and a broken phrase or two of this hymn. . . . I suggest that we keep our seats as we sing this hymn softly."

And then the packed congregation sang all the verses: "Be still my soul, the Lord is on thy side. . . ."

Next, Mr. W.E. McLaren spoke. He had been interned while serving as the business agent of a British shipping company in China, but he was uniquely qualified to talk about sportsmanship and Eric Liddell. Twenty-two years before, he had played for Scotland on the Rugby International XV with A. Leslie Gracie and Eric.

Mr. McLaren told how opponents in rugby would often "lay for" Eric, but he would never retaliate. ". . . his method was invariable—he merely played better rugby and made them look like second-raters." He told how Eric never gave up in a race, even after getting a slow start, and how athletic fame did not turn his head.

Next came Mr. C.H.B. Longman, Headmaster at the Tientsin Anglo-Chinese College. Eric had lived with him during those lonely months between his family's departure in 1929 and his first furlough in 1931. He told about the wonderful, loving home of Reverend and Mrs. James D. Liddell at Siaochang, where he had visited in 1912; about the way Eric, as the new faculty member at the TACC, had encouraged the staff to open school in September of 1925, when a student boycott was threatened to make the missionaries appear impotent. Mr. Longman finished with a description of Eric's Christian character, which he said was the reason Eric was so universally respected in the camp.

"One of the best and tersest injunctions of St. Paul to his friends was, 'Run to win!' In the spiritual race Eric was always in training, always in form, and always ran true to form. He ran to win, and he won gloriously, didn't he?"

Following Mr. Longman came Miss Annie Buchan. She told of Eric's work as a rural missionary in the Hopei Province, beginning in the fall of 1937. Many of the listeners, who had known Eric as a teacher and counselor of the internee children, had no idea of his work as an itinerant pastor during the Japanese occupation. Again and again, listeners were amazed to hear accounts of actions that would have resulted in decorations for valor, had Eric been a military man.

Last, Mr. P.A. Bruce, Headmaster of the Chefoo School, told about Eric's work as teacher, sports director, and Christian youth leader in the Weihsien camp. He told several incidents in which Eric carried other people's responsibilities without mentioning it, and donated his own personal resources to the children's needs. The gold watch given to Eric by the City of Edinburgh, it seems, had been sold quietly to buy needed supplies for the internees.

Readings at the memorial service were selected from the Sermon on the Mount, and from 1 Corinthians 13, St. Paul's hymn to perfect love. When the service was over, a shock and a certain lethargy set in among some of the internees of the Weihsien camp. While Eric would have wanted them to carry on as before, there was the inescapable fact that a seemingly indestructible person had died with apparent suddenness. If an Olympic champion who could still outrun the fastest youth in the camp, a man who exemplified Christ in his daily affairs, could be snatched away, who might be next? It was a natural, very human emotion.

About two weeks after the memorial service at Weihsien, while the Red Cross notice of Eric's death was still wending its way towards Florence at Toronto, another Olympic champion died at Iwo Jima. He was Colonel Takeichi, Baron Nishi, commander of the tank regiment, the Japanese officer who had expressed hope for world peace after winning the *Prix de Nations* equestrian event at Los Angeles in 1932. While some said he participated in a mass *hari-kiri* action by Japanese military men as the U.S. forces closed in, Colonel Nishi's wife would always maintain that he died honorably in battle.

As for the Red Cross death notice, the copy to Jenny passed through North Africa en route to Scotland. Red Cross services in the North African theater of operations were directed by William Stevenson, Eric's U.S. quarter mile opponent in 1924.

In April, while U.S., British, and Russian forces were converging upon the heartland of Germany, Florence Liddell had a strange experience. She imagined that Eric was standing behind her, and she could feel his strength. She asked him if he were all right, and he said, "It's okay, Flossie," using the private name by which he called her when he teased her.

It was an especially cruel blow to her, therefore, when two friends came to the door of her parents' home on May 2 where she was staying with the girls. They had been asked by the Toronto office of the Red Cross to carry the sad message of Eric's death. Florence had two brothers serving with the Canadian armed forces, and she was not sure which member of her family would be the subject of the news she somehow knew was going to be tragic. When they told her, she was simply dumbfounded. She had not even known that Eric was seriously ill.

Just one week after the day when Florence knew that Eric would never return, millions thrilled to the news of the imminent return of their men from overseas when Germany surrendered. Florence suffered from emotional depression, for her grief came during her country's most jubilant moment, and many did not consider missionary internees to have been part of the war effort. But always, Eric's face and voice appeared to her, reminding her of the three girls he had left in her care. Later, friends from the Weihsien camp would tell her how Eric regretted the limited time they had spent together. And, being a daughter of the missionary service, Florence would always see her marriage to Eric as a treasure, counting the blessings of the seven hectic years they had spent together in China, Scotland, and Cànada.

In May, while people in Edinburgh, Glasgow, Toronto, and other Allied cities thanked God for the end of the Nazi military power, memorial services were conducted for Eric that set in motion the legacy by which he is remembered. The story at Weihsien, however, came to an end in August of 1945.

After the dropping of the atomic bombs on Hiroshima and Nagasaki, the Allies feared that the Japanese might misread the signals. What if they took this awesome demonstration of military power as an invitation to an even more fanatic defense of every square inch of territory? What if they retaliated by murdering the prisoners and internees in their camps? General Douglas MacArthur, Supreme Commander of Allied Forces in the Pacific, was knowledgeable of Asian politics and psychology; so was General George C. Marshall in Washington, D.C. The dropping of the bomb was calculated to reduce the quantity of both Japanese and Allied human slaughter that would accompany an invasion of the Japanese mainland, where the military fanatics of the Tojo regime held power.

The internees at Weihsien did not know about the atomic bombs being dropped in early August, but they did know that a major military operation had taken place. The Japanese military officers were talking about a sudden departure, and they were secretive where they had once been informative about camp policy. The internees could not know of two other policy considerations at work on the limited Allied military resources in China.

First, Lt. General Albert C. Wedemeyer had impressed upon the administration in Washington, D.C., with General MacArthur's strong concurrence, that a new threat existed in China. Much of the Chinese military power in northern China was really the Red Army, who had given clear intentions of overthrowing the Nationalist government as soon as the Japanese threat was gone. Second, the Soviet Union was hastily moving troops toward Manchuria and the northern islands of Japan, signaling that they intended to take advantage of the Axis demise by carving out their own eastern empire. Third, when Japan surrendered, there would be a breakdown of control over Japanese troops. Who could give assurance that Japanese soldiers, steeped in fanatical notions of military supremacy and racial superiority, would not slaughter the military prisoners and the civilian internees?

One morning, Miss Annie Buchan had a surprise in her hospital ward. Cases of canned fruit juice came crashing through the window, flattening the tins and even injuring some of her patients. Curiously, at that moment, the Japanese guards were not at the towers. People ran out into the yard and saw that the cans of juice were coming from the sky, dropped by a reconnaissance plane with U.S. Army Air Corps markings.

Later in the day, a small flight of C-47 transports appeared with fighter escort. They circled the camp, and, on the second pass, put out a squad of paratroopers who cautiously secured the camp's guard towers. Then came bundles and bundles of foodstuffs and relief supplies, also delivered by parachute. And the next day, an emergency logistics and security force arrived.

The U.S. Army major commanding the detachment decided on a bluff, for his detachment was no match for the Japanese security force at Weihsien. He walked to the gate, ordered the guard to send out his commanding officer, and assumed a non-combative posture.

When the Japanese major arrived, the U.S. detachment simply walked in, and the commander told his Japanese opposite to have his men put their weapons in the arms room. Then he held a quick meeting with the camp committee heads and learned the priorities about internees who needed emergency care. The Japanese soldiers marched quietly away to the city of Weihsien, minus their weapons, fearful of reprisal by Chinese civilians.

One might ask why so few troops were used to rescue the internees. The U.S. Army's own elite 11th Airborne Division even had nervous moments securing General MacArthur's arrival in mainland Japan. The theater command in China had mainly support aircraft and Chinese troops. An amphibious force of U.S. Marines stood offshore near Chefoo but did not land, because a strategic decision had been made to ferry the Nationalist Army northward in U.S. aircraft, and for the U.S. forces not to engage the Red Army in China. Consequently, the rescue of the internees was a delicate political-military maneuver, carried out with great skill.

The British missionaries and civilians were taken, after three weeks at Weihsien for recuperation, to Tsingtao. From there, they were carried aboard H.M.S. *Geneva* to Hong Kong. The American logistical staff cared for them, but the seasonal storms created high seas and resulted in a miserable trip.

A surprise awaited authorities upon the ship's arrival at Hong Kong. The experience was similar to that of American missionary personnel liberated by U.S. forces at Manila. The surprise was that the civilians were actually in better physical shape than had been expected. The Japanese military forces had regarded *military* prisoners as persons already deceased, and as morally dishonored for having surrendered. Consequently, abuse of U.S., British, French, Dutch, and Chinese prisoners of war by Japanese guards was extreme. Most prisoners died, and those who were liberated were pitiful to behold, their health ruined and their lives shortened. The missionaries and the other civilian internees, by contrast, were treated better, in terms of having management over their own compounds and access to a higher level of nutrition. So the missionaries from Weihsien received little sympathy and even some resentment from their own countrymen at Hong Kong. Their effort at maintaining a cheerful demeanor were viewed by some military men as a failure to take the war seriously. Had Eric survived to participate in the release from Japanese captivity, he would have been hurt, as he was by people who called him a traitor for not running in Sunday heats at the Olympic Games; but undoubtedly he would have prayed for understanding of the situation.

The British missionaries made it home by Christmas aboard the H.M.S. *Oxfordshire,* a hospital ship. They were thankful for their deliverance, and because of their longer exposure to World War II in Asia, they probably understood, better than Americans, how fortunate the world was for the Japanese decision to surrender following the bombing of Hiroshima and Nagasaki.

General Douglas MacArthur was the dominant military personality throughout the Allied victory, and he was an admirer of sports in general, and a significant advocate of the Olympic Games. As Superintendent at West Point, he showed awareness of the concept of Arnoldism in education that had been so influential in Eric Liddell's life. MacArthur's own words on the subject were mounted in bronze letters upon the walls at the West Point gymnasium: "Upon the fields of friendly strife are sown the seeds that, upon other days, on other fields, will bear the fruits of victory."

In 1928, as Chairman of the U.S. Olympic Committee, he recorded his opinion of the Olympic movement and its moral values in his report after the Amsterdam Games. "The [Olympic] athletic code," wrote MacArthur, "had come down to us from even before the age of chivalry and knighthood. It embraces the highest moral laws and will stand the test of any ethics or philosophies ever promulgated for the uplift of man. Its requirements are for the things that are right, and its restraints are from the things that are wrong."

Eric would have agreed with this opinion. And MacArthur evidently grasped the kind of Armageddon struggle that would have occurred if an assault force, primarily American, had struck the Japanese mainland in the fall of 1945. Had the atomic bomb not been dropped, twelve American divisions with supporting troops would have been expended, just to get a military foothold on the southern islands. The operation was code-named OLYMPIC. The 1940 Olympic Games originally had been scheduled for Tokyo and were reassigned to Helsinki when Japan invaded China. This was a sad page in the history of the Olypmic movement. But the world is fortunate indeed that Operation OLYMPIC of 1945 was cancelled because Japan surrendered as a result of President Harry S Truman's decision to drop the atomic bomb.

The death of Eric Liddell is part of a greater sequence of events in the final days of World War II. Eric's life and death took place amid the clash of mighty armies, navies, and air armadas in the world's most intense, most clear-cut struggle between good and evil. His life was one of many Christian sacrifices, joyfully and humbly offered. In August of 1945, the legacy of Eric Liddell would be left to those dearest to him in Scotland and Canada. Eventually, this legacy would include movies, books, religious organizations, sporting trophies, memorial facilities, and, to be sure, legends that are not all true.

The legacy of Eric Liddell began in the snow at Weihsien as each person learned of his death. The spiritual leaders in the camp encouraged those who grieved by helping them to look at those ideals and truths by which Eric lived. Meanwhile, the same Scottish ministers, athletes, and community leaders who surrounded Eric in his period of Olympic and student evangelical glory set the tone of his legacy through a series of memorial services in May 1945.

The churchmen in Scotland waited just a few days so that the first memorial service could be held in Toronto. There, Florence and her family and a large congregation assembled at the Carlton Street United Church. The two principal speakers had both known Eric during his missionary work, and the service occurred just when news of the German surrender was being felt in Toronto homes.

One speaker was the Reverend George K. King, a missionary serving in China who had been interned. "At Weihsien Internment Camp," said the Reverend King, "there was a quiet room for meditation and prayer; [Eric] was often there. It is only natural that his ability in guiding and inspiring boys should be recognized. It was not unusual to see half a dozen youngsters starting off on a prowl. One wondered what mischief they had in mind, and looked to identify the leader; then, recognizing Eric Liddell, felt assured that with such a guide only good could result."

The other speaker, the Reverend T.T. Faichney, was a Scot living in Ontario. He had spent several years as a missionary in China, where he had been minister of the Union Church in Tientsin while Eric was on the staff of the TACC. "Eric was absolutely true and genuine in everything he said and did," began the Reverend Faichney. He went on to share an anecdote.

While Eric was Sunday School teacher of the missionary children at the Union Church, he had taught the pupils that the trait called "sincerity" had Latin roots. "Sincere," Eric had said, "derives from *sine ceres,* meaning, literally, 'without wax'." Later on, Eric had shown Reverend Faichney a letter, written to him by a pupil who evidently took some notes on the origins of the word "sincerity," for he ended the letter, "Yours, without wax." Eric's eyes twinkled as he showed the letter.

"In 1937," continued Reverend Faichney, "when the decision was made that [Eric] should go from his teaching ministry in The Anglo-Chinese College in Tientsin to rural work down-country, some of us very close to him . . . did not feel that it was right, but Eric accepted it, and today we know that he was right.

"Everything that Eric did, he did well. . . . I have here with me a small booklet entitled, *The Sermon on the Mount,* Sunday School lessons prepared for the teachers of Union Church Sunday School by Eric. It is the best thing that I have on the Sermon on the Mount in my library. Going through it, one marvels at his erudition, his wide reading as shown in the bibliography and his spiritual perception."

Reverend Faichney closed with one of the few evaluations extant of Eric's theology, by a pastoral colleague. "[Eric's] definition of the Kingdom of Heaven was the simplest and most satisfying of any I know. 'The Kingdom is where the King reigns,' said Eric one day in the Sunday School. 'If He is reigning in my heart, then the Kingdom of Heaven has come to me!' [Eric] had that Kingdom of Heaven quality of life; in his serenity and peace, it was expressed in his smiling countenance. He walked with God. He was one of the 'terrible meek,' for he sought nothing for himself, but sensitive to others' needs, with great understanding, infinite patience, and a saving sense of humour, he gave to others, both Chinese and foreigners, that same quality of Kingdom of Heaven serenity and goodness."

On May 27, the city of Edinburgh with Eric's family paid their formal tribute at the Morningside Congregational Church. The building has been changed a little, but one can still see the neighborhood where Eric and his family lived in furnished flats during his first two years at the University of Edinburgh. Morningside has produced a whole roster of powerful overseas missionaries, and in 1945, there were still active members who remembered Eric's student years there.

The congregation numbered over one thousand, and there was standing room only. Rob, Jenny, and Ernest were there, along with senior representatives of the Scottish Amateur Athletics Association and the London Missionary Society. Headmaster George Robertson of George Watson's College in Edinburgh gave one tribute; he had been Eric's beloved and influential Headmaster down at Eltham College. A second eulogy came from the Reverend D.P. Thomson, the man who brought Eric into the Glasgow Students' Evangelical Union at Armadale, April 1923. The Reverend Thomson went on to become the principal architect of transmitting Eric's legacy to the world. The third memorial speaker at the Edinburgh service was Duncan Macleod Wright, the British Marathon champion and Scotland's best-known Olympic athlete following Eric's departure from the athletics scene.

On the following day, May 28, Reverend Thomson and Dr. Rob Liddell went to Glasgow for what was to be the largest and most symbolic tribute paid to Eric until the 1980s. Before the turn of the century, James D. Liddell was ordained at the Dundas Street Congregational Church, seat of the Congregational Union of Scotland. In 1925, Eric had made his unforgettable departure speech there in late June, following the triple crown victory in his last track meet. Now, the Reverend James M. Calder, Chairman (chief ecclesiastical authority) of the Congregational Union of Scotland, presided over a turnaway crowd that included the top athletics and evangelical names in the land.

William Struth, Manager of the Glasgow Celtics Football Club, made a rare public speech that was carried by the British Broadcasting Corporation at home and abroad. "[Eric] deliberately sacrificed a fine chance to one Olympic title because of his religious convictions. He just as certainly put aside a career of brilliance and affluence to serve his Master in the most practical of all forms of Christianity."

These opinions were coming from a man who was the Scottish sporting world's equivalent of the Dallas Cowboys' legendary coach Tom Landry in the United States. "Sport gave to Eric Liddell its highest honours; nevertheless, it is true to say that he honoured sport rather than sport honouring him." Struth went on to say that Scotland did not, as yet, know much about the details of Eric's final years, but he offered one judgment.

"[Eric's] life was perhaps a short one; but his work, as he clearly saw it, and, as we believe, divinely inspired, carried out away from the applause of the crowd, will remain a source of inspiration to many. In these days of exaggerated hero worship and publicity for sports champions, Eric Liddell's example reminds us to put things in their proper perspective. Sport to him was sport—not the be-all and end-all—and success in it did not prevent him from picking out the things spiritual from the things temporal. His was an example which must have helped others to make a similar choice."

Duncan Macleod Wright had last seen Eric on a running track at Toronto in 1932 when Eric was visiting with some members of the British Olympic team. "On behalf of the athletes of Scotland," Duncan said, "I wish to pay a humble tribute to our late colleague, Eric Liddell. . . . His shining example on the sports field attracted many young lads to our sport. People came from all parts to see this Christian athlete, who ran not for prize or glory, but for love of the sport."

Then the Marathon champ noted one of the key dimensions of Eric's character.

"We could go to any international gathering with a jauntiness in our step—we knew that our men would do well. Eric was greater than an athlete: he was a Crusade. He was without doubt the most glorious runner I have ever seen.

"Never has there been a greater need for a man with such a high moral and virile Christian character like Eric Liddell, to be set as an example to our young people." Duncan's challenge here was taken up by the men of the GSEU, who spoke next.

The Reverend Robert Dobbie and the Reverend D.P. Thomson were two of the five founders, back in 1922, of the Glasgow Students' Evangelical Union. Reverend Dobbie reminisced upon the year when Eric studied theology at the Scottish Congregational College at 29 Hope Terrace.

"His presence immediately suggested a gentle and radiant life. One thought spontaneously of Chaucer's line, 'He was a very parfit, gentle Knight.' To gentleness he added the gaiety and gladness of a Christian soul. Every grace he offered at table was a song of thanksgiving.

"This fellowship with God, was, indeed, the nerve center of his life. I can see him now, reading his evening portion in the College Common

Room, quietly browsing in pastures from which the spiritual life of all the students benefited, marking passages which impressed him: his face aglow with God. To this delight in the spiritual treasury of the past he added his own deep life of prayer.

"On one occasion, contemplating the contrast between his international fame and his modesty, we asked him how he had been able to surmount the temptations to egotism in his continuous exposure to public praise. He replied, with classic, moving simplicity, 'I prayed about it.' With true spiritual discernment he recognized his danger, and by the grace of God not only conquered it, but even turned it to his spiritual advantage.

"His life was characterized by an amazing mastery. In large measure he merited the tribute Samuel Johnson paid to [Oliver] Goldsmith, that he touched nothing which he did not adorn. His spiritual mastery, born of utter renunciation to Jesus Christ, and a passion for perfection, expressed itself in a character in which the closest scrutiny could detect no flaw. 'He was a very parfit, gentle Knight.' "

The Reverend D.P. Thomson presented the other eulogy, which he soon developed into a kind of mini-biography of Eric's life. Immediately following the memorial services and time spent with Eric's family, Reverend Thomson set to work on a very constructive project that had a twofold benefit. He formed a national committee of leaders from the religious, educational, business, and sporting sector to commemorate Eric's life, and to provide for Florence and the girls.

A series of public memorials was set in motion, with a collection taken up for Eric's family. Reverend Thomson wrote a little pamphlet in the form of a tract, a common practice by the churches which had a large overseas missionary commitment. A committee in Canada cooperated with the committee in Scotland in selling the pamphlet, and in conducting fund raising memorial assemblies. By this means, enough money was raised that Florence could care for herself and the girls in a modest but dignified manner.

Eric had once gone far out of his way to appear at the benefit track meets sponsored by the professional Association Football teams. Now, the Association Football leaders remembered Eric and returned the gesture. Their fund raising events, conducted in the form of Eric Liddell memorial rallies, gathered funds to assist Eric's family and enough to establish an Eric Liddell Challenge Trophy. This award began in 1946 and today is the pinnacle of sporting excellence for the top track and field athlete of Scotland, chosen from among some 150 schools.

As a memorial fund campaign was in full swing, the Reverend D.P. Thomson learned in the fall of 1946 that the amateur rugby teams in the border towns were planning a religious rally as a United Student Campaign. Eric was the honoree, Reverend Thomson was the principal speaker, and thirteen Scottish International rugby veterans participated in the Sunday afternoon service at St. Paul's Parish Church in the border town rugby stronghold, Galashiels. D.P. Thomson, by this time, had consolidated his presentations about Eric into one that focused on the six cornerstones of Eric Liddell's life.

First came the home in which Eric was raised. Anyone who knew the quality of the early family life provided by James and Mary Liddell knew the origin of Eric's ideals and inspiration. Second was the quality of the boarding school in which Eric spent eleven years. Honesty, purity, and fair play were three cardinal traits that he learned at Eltham College.

Third of Eric's main strengths, according to the Reverend Thomson, was his concentration, "a quiet resoluteness and calm that were very impressive to watch." Fourth was Eric's sense of duty. Reverend Thomson illustrated this trait by telling the story of how Eric had leaped across open water at Port Arthur to catch the steamer back to Tientsin, having first honored the national anthems of Britain and France.

Above all these traits, said Thomson, came "the stand he took for Jesus Christ;" here, there is a point of difference. The Reverend Thomson, who did so much for Eric's memory and family, had an unfortunate tendency to equate the beginning of Eric's Christian commitment with the April 1923 public witnessing appearance at Armadale. With the advantages of time and distance, it becomes clear that Armadale was Eric's conversion to public evangelism, but that his commitment to the missionary service long pre-dated Armadale. And fifth, according to the Reverend Thomson's summary of Eric's traits, was "the quest which he pursued so resolutely to the very end, for a fuller knowledge of God and a closed approximation to His mind and will." Certainly no one would dispute Thomson's judgment on this point.

As Britain set about the arduous post-war reconstruction and healing process, there was one knight who could not remain inside the castle walls. Miss Annie Buchan bade farewell to Peterhead once more and in 1947 returned to China. The war between the Nationalist and Communist forces was in full force. No one will ever know if Eric Liddell would have returned for one more period of service in China, or if he would have taken a "sphere" in western Canada. Furthermore, we do not know Eric's views on the Communist Revolution in China; we can only view a bit of this realm through Miss Annie's eyes.

She managed to serve again as a missionary nurse in China for over two years. The extreme anti-Christian virulence that burst out during the Boxer Rebellion was more diffused, because the Communist Revolution, while violent and vicious, was a combined political and spiritual movement with a positive ideology of its own. Miss Annie was well aware of the purges, the killings, the mass executions of selected social classes; but she also perceived that those who led the Communist Revolution were looking for solutions to human dilemmás.

The key to Annie's survival was to make things appear as if the revolutionaries were doing the good works, a tactic of applied Christian love that she had mastered during the Japanese occupation. Thus, on one occasion when a high official in the Communist Party required a medical procedure that only the British missionary staff knew how to do, she helped the medical team to carry it out and thanked the authorities for their fine work! In the end, the Revolution, and its bitter period of consolidating power, could not co-exist with a foreign moral presence, even as gentle a presence as Miss Annie. By 1950, she was back in Peterhead, ministering to the needy and the sick in a Scottish fishing town.

Relationships between the Christian West and post-Revolutionary China were never entirely broken. Missionary work never entirely ceased and, by the 1970s, there was evidence that Chinese Christians were a viable moral force. In 1975, a "Love China First" rally was held in Manila, devoted to evangelical work and paying homage to such servants as James Hudson Taylor. In 1982, the new Constitution of the People's Republic of China proclaimed religious freedom, coupled with guarantees against both repression for religious practice and enforced practice against one's individual will.

One of Eric's final roommates at the Weihsien camp was Mr. John Hoyte, today a successful electronics manufacturer in California. Hoyte's grandfather trained for the missionary service at a Dwight Moody "Athletes for Christ" camp, and the family did yeoman service in China. After the liberation, Hoyte combined his love of history, and his flair for publicity by re-enacting Hannibal's march across the Alps with war elephants, then writing a successful book about it.

How Eric would have chuckled over his friend's exploit! But John Hoyte had bigger plans to commemorate Eric's legacy. In August, 1985, he led forty of the Weihsien camp survivors back to China for a reunion. They found the city had grown out to cover the former compound in the countryside, and sadly, the cemetery where Eric was buried is now a paved city street. But the Chinese government officials cooperated fully, even acknowledged the bravery of the Christian missionaries in trying to help their Chinese parishioners.

In 1947, Eltham College was expanding and bought a new dormitory at 33 Grove Park Road. In July of 1924, Eric had come down to London to run in the post-Olympic Relays, and the welcome at his alma mater had been thunderous. Now, he was the overwhelming choice to be honored by the dedication of a building. Liddell House was named in his honor, and the boys who live in it are proudly aware of Eric's career and values. Another son of Eltham who brought great honor after World War II was A. Leslie Gracie, Eric's old partner on the Eltham and Scottish Internationalist rugby three-quarter wing. Gracie did not have to perform combat service again in World War II, due both to age and previous combat service; but he came out of the second war again highly decorated, a Knight of the British Empire.

In the summer of 1948, the British Olympic Committee and the City of London agreed to host the XIVth Olympiad, despite critical shortages of money and facilities. Meat rationing was still on, and many citizens wondered if Britons needed to be spending money to host foreign athletes. Eric's old friend Harold Abrahams worked hard for public acceptance of the Games. Philip Baker, now known as "Noel-Baker," lent his spiritual and political influence as a senior Member of Parliment. The London Games of 1948 would have pleased Eric tremendously. They were conducted economically, apolitically, and with great technical excellence save for a few errors in the boxing competition management.

The Invocation at the Inauguration of U.S. President Harry S. Truman was given by the Chaplain of the U.S. Senate, the Reverend Peter Marshall. Just a few weeks later, overwork and a massive heart attack would end the earthly ministry of the dynamic Scot who functioned as a much beloved, post-World War II Isaiah in Washington, D.C. Eric always taught that the finest treasures grow from out of the worst tragedies; Peter Marshall's untimely death led his widow, Catherine, to take up the pen, and she would shortly become one of the world's most beloved Christian writers.

Richard Todd and Jean Peters created the beautiful film portrait of Peter and Catherine Marshall in 1955, *A Man Called Peter*. The men of Annapolis had never forgotten Peter's famous 1941 graduation sermon. When actor Richard Todd gave part of the sermon in the Annapolis Chapel to be captured on film, the midshipmen volunteer actors playing the role of the 1941 congregation insisted that he finish it. And all of this legacy stems from a visit between a discouraged Scottish college student and Eric Liddell. When Peter was rejected for the China missionary service, he dug in more deeply—seminary in Decatur, Georgia; odd jobs to earn money; devoted parish ministry—and onward to the Chaplaincy of the United States Senate!

In 1951, Florenze Mackenzie Liddell married Mr. Murray Hall of Binbrook. Thanks to the rallying-around of the missionary service veterans in 1945-1946, she had been free to marry for love. Florence and Murray enjoyed a long, happy marriage. Murray brought three children of his own into the marriage, and he and Florence had a daughter named Jeannie.

During the 1950s the Soviet Union re-entered the Olympic Games, and Eric would have been pleased to see the growth in participation. He would not have approved of the political grandstanding between the communist and democratic nations, nor of the medal counting. He disagreed fundamentally with the kind of thinking that made amateur Olympians into professionals, either through government stipends or private sector donations. And it would have been his way to suggest several practical ideas to ameliorate this unwholesome trend, with a disarming little grin on his face, his eyes twinkling. Typically, his suggestions for strengthing genuine Olympic amateurism would have at first appeared simplistic, but, upon close examination, would have revealed profound thought.

In 1959, Phil Noel-Baker went to Stockholm to receive the Nobel Peace Prize. Forty-seven years before, while Eric was a school boy athlete at Eltham College, Phil had certified the British Olympic team lists at Stockholm as captain. His award was for authorship of a meticulously researched plan for world disarmament, and he immediately donated the prize money to the United Nations Society. It was Phil Baker who went to school in Philadelphia, who was inspired by the same motto that inspired Eric at the University of Pennsylvania, who demonstrated these principles on the track, even though Eric once said it might have been Phil Baker who sent the bagpipers marching before the beginning of the 400-meter race!

In 1954, the young Dr. Billy Graham came to Britain for a televised Easter Crusade, the first such event to be broadcast live with sight and sound. The Graham organization went to the man who had put Eric Liddell on the public platform. The Reverend D.P. Thomson trained 600 Scottish religious counselors to support the campaign, and Dr. Graham was hailed in Scotland in the tradition of Dwight Moody, Henry Drummond, the "Cambridge Seven," and, of course, Eric Liddell. In 1955, Dr. Graham repeated the campaign at Glasgow.

In June of 1961, Christian athlete leaders in Edinburgh dedicated the Eric Liddell Memorial Room at St. Ninian's Conference and Training Centre. Representatives from clubs, colleges, and secondary schools all over Scotland came in for the memorial exercises. The facility was installed in a vacated church building on Fountainhall Road. In addition to serving as a meeting hall for Christian youth activities, the St. Ninian's Centre maintained displays of memorabilia about Eric and his career. Sadly, this facility was destroyed by a fire and has not been replaced.

In 1965, the Reverend D.P. Thomson spoke at the founding of the Eric Liddell Club for Boys at Crieff, in Perthshire County. The club offers a full program of sports and religious activities, and it continues Eric's work as he would have done it in contemporary society. In 1970, Edinburgh was selected as the site for the British Empire Games, and Reverend Thomson saw a tremendous opportunity to project Eric Liddell before the world again. Coupled with the Edinburgh Summer Festival, Thomson saw that the Empire Games would bring tens of thousands of people to Scotland's historic old capital.

Thomson had ministered to sailors during the First World War, to workers and students in the 1920s, to thousands of soldiers during World War II. While his career was different from Eric's, his theology and personality were a strong influence in Eric's life. And due to his interest in the legacy of Eric Liddell, Thomson assembled all the biographical materials he could find into a book called *Scotland's Greatest Athlete: The Eric Liddell Story.* He had it published privately at Crieff, and it was sold through church rallies and benefit meetings.

After 1970, the book sparked a resurgence of interest in Eric, and Reverend Thomson published a revised version in 1971 called *Eric Liddell, Athlete and Missionary.* This, too, sold out quickly; the proceeds went to support youth evangelical work. And the 1970s were a changing of the guard among Eric's family and friends, most of whom survived to see the success of Thomson's 1970 book.

By the end of the decade, most of the family from Eric's generation would be gone. Florence's second husband Murray Hall passed away; while Eric and Florence only had girls, Eric's grandchildren numbered six boys and three girls. Jenny's husband, Dr. Charles Somerville, passed away. He and Jenny had two daughters, both married and close to their mother. Ernest Liddell died, following years of serious health disorders. Far out in Australia, Dr. Rob Liddell died while on an extended visit with his son, who also became a physician.

In the 1970s, many people felt that the media—films, magazines, television, radio—were wasting a great opportunity to elevate civilization and were, in fact, contributing to a mood of cynicism. One is hard pressed to name a successful media offering in the 1970s that is not dependent in major part upon sarcasm, violence, explicit sex, or social deviancy in some form. Further, British moviegoers were showing some preference for a certain genre of cynical, materialistic film produced in America.

British movie producer David Puttnam almost single-handedly restored the power of British cinema at the turnstile. Pictures like *Duellists; Bugsy Malone; That'll Be the Day; Brother, Can You Spare a Dime?* and *Midnight Express* brought out the viewers with their technical and artistic excellence, but they featured the same kinds of hard-boiled themes that originated in Hollywood. Puttnam was troubled by criticism and sought a vehicle to portray a moral kind of metaphor and, hopefully, not go bankrupt in the process. He found his theme in a pre-1980 edition of Bill Henry's *Approved History of the Olympic Games,* where there was a sketchy and historically inaccurate portrayal of Harold Abrahams and Eric Liddell at the 1924 Paris Olympic Games.

Puttnam hired Colin Welland to do his script. The Reverend John Keddie, a Scottish triple jump champion and minister who follows in Eric's tradition, did much research on the sporting details. Mrs. Jenny Somerville cooperated mightily, even after discovering that she was to be re-cast as an ill-humored sister who opposed Eric's running on the grounds that it conflicted with his religious work! Air Canada flew Heather and Maureen over for the Scottish premiere on April 13, 1981. Patricia remained at home to care for her mother who was not well. Jenny attended, as did Allan Wells, the Scottish winner of the 100-meter sprint at the 1980 Moscow Olympics. Wells had told the press how he "won it for Eric" and showed Jenny his medal.

Members of Harold Abrahams' family also attended, again recognizing that Harold had been significantly altered to create an artistic tension within the story. There was a formal presentation of the cast and the families of the principle characters in *Chariots of Fire* to Queen Elizabeth, the Queen Mother. Edinburgh University set loose a series of public events honoring Eric; one of these was the dedication of the Eric Liddell Memorial Gymnasium. The Reverend D.P. Thomson, who once orchestrated Eric's affairs in Edinburgh, had died, but others like John Keddie took up the task.

Cambridge University, portrayed in *Chariots of Fire* as a quaint training ground for young men of religious Anglo-Saxon prejudice, was less enthusiastic about *Chariots of Fire,* and, in fact, much of the footage was made at St. Andrews, where Eric had run some of his finest Inter-University track meets. Bill Stevenson, who ran for the U.S. 4 x 400 meter relay team at Paris in 1924, stated emphatically that "anti-Semitism did not exist on the British Olympic team." But David Puttnam has given the world a priceless gift, one which transcends any momentary criticism about the politics and characterizations of his movie.

The script, the acting, and the music of *Chariots of Fire* are artistic gems, richly deserving of the Academy Awards they received. Ian Charleson's portrayal of Eric, minus a few changes in historical detail, is highly accurate; Rob and Eric's father are superbly done. The real Jenny appears in the fictional cameo scene where the movie Eric is thundering like Isaiah about how God makes rules and rulers, while the movie Harold and teammates flounder about on the track at the Stade Colombes.

But these details pale beside the central point: David Puttnam has created a vehicle by which to portray the magnificence of Eric Liddell to the cynical, stimuli-overloaded world of the 1980s. While Eric would dislike the publicity, he would praise God for seeing the Christian evangelical effort put so beautifully before the public. David Puttnam has recreated artistically a concept of athletics that was known and advocated by Plato, St. Paul, Coubertin, the "Cambridge Seven," and the Yale Athletes for Christ. His story vehicle was Eric Liddell.

Hot in the wake of *Chariots of Fire* came Sally Magnusson's book *The Flying Scotsman.* Sally did the world more yeoman service by capturing the details of Eric's family, by sorting out fact from screen fiction in *Chariots of Fire,* and, most of all, by putting Eric's message into millions of homes. And next came a beautiful BBC television documentary on Eric, capturing Florence on film with priceless anecdotes about her first husband.

As the theme song to *Chariots of Fire* and the actors from the movie began to appear on television commercials, major evangelical leaders grasped the significance of Eric's life and of the world's need for Eric's influence. The Billy Graham Crusade, through its Wide World Productions, acquired the rights to *Chariots of Fire* as inspirational material and began scripting their own movie about Eric's years as a missionary in China. Tentatively, the title is *Burning Gold,* and thorough research has gone into the story. Thus, the missionary-evangelical community once again comes together; Eric's name is linked with a roster of superstars of the nineteenth and twentieth century.

And so we come to the question: why is the world so interested in a man who refused to run an Olympic event on Sunday, when others did the same thing? Why such interest in a missionary who was never even the chief executive of a missionary station? Why do we think of Eric with names like James Hudson Taylor, Dwight L. Moody, David Livingstone, James Gilmour, Henry Drummond, and Billy Graham? We could more easily compare him with America's hero Olympian Glenn Cunningham, who recovered from massive leg burns to become the nation's greatest miler, a silver medal Olympian, holder of an earned doctorate, and stepfather to ten thousand homeless boys on a farm in Kansas. Glenn, too, preaches and lives by St. Paul's hymn to unquestioning love, the ringing, timeless message of 1 Corinthians 13.

First, at the theological level, Eric is vital because he was both a theoretician and a practitioner. *Disciplines of the Christian Life* (1985) is Abingdon Publisher's meticulous version of Eric's 1942 *Manual for Christian Discipleship*. Edited by Mary Ruth Howes, herself a China missionary internee during World War II, its galley proofs were done just in time for Florence to see before she died. *Disciplines* gives us Eric's mature theology; his adaptive work in fitting the tough, overlapping Christian mandates to real life are intellectually brilliant, far beyond the worth of an abstract theory. His committed Christian life in the practice of these lessons has few peers in the twentieth century.

Second, at the social level, the world needs the standard embodied by Eric Liddell. His winsome, delightful personality is a clear role model, a statement in practical Christian reality. People who find it awkward or unsophisticated to be positive witnesses for their faith will discover multiple paths to Christian witness and practice by examining Eric's life.

Third, Eric is a theological and political bridge between East and West. Christians of the west cannot ignore China, whose people number nearly a third of the world's population. Christians cannot dismiss Communism merely by saying that it is evil, for it is a form of social evangelism that captures hearts and minds. Eric, in his call to China, in his brilliant translation of a Scottish championship athletics career into an exemplary ministry of several levels, becomes a bridge. His work makes it possible for others to cross over. How Eric would have glowed at the winsome Chinese Olympic athletes at Los Angeles in July and August of 1984! How he would sparkle to the reports of missionaries in China today, of Chinese Christians who are continuing his work! Were he alive today, he would glory in the upcoming XXIVth Olympiad at Seoul, the first Games on the Asian mainland.

Fourth, Eric offers an intelligent and sensitive solution to the dilemma of the Christian democracies who, in their enthusiasm to separate church and state and to be impartial before all religious beliefs, have reduced the moral choices at national level to simplistic political platitudes. Eric was very aware that there is a place in the order of things for politics. And he had an answer, a well thought out moral answer to the dilemma of the liberal-conservative debate that often reduces Christian policy choices to a simplistic "be nice or be tough" stance. "Righteousness," said Eric, "is often too hard. It needs the softening power of mercy. Mercy is often too soft. To be merciful towards the failings of others without a moral protest at the heart of the mercy ends in looseness."

Fifth, Eric offers a personal friendship with himself and with God. He leads us to the way of Jesus, teaching us to be full of compassion but also willing to stand up for what is right, to demand the best in ourselves. And he lives it all, does it all, describes it in an easily visualized, contemporary metaphor.

Eric Liddell was God's gentle knight. He was the perfect example of the Olympic amateur athlete. He was a serious, powerful theologian, and he practiced a vigorous, committed Christian life. He invites us to open our hearts to our fellow human beings, to open our ears to God's Word, to extend our hand in friendship. Then he suggests that we get our heads well back and set off upon the great track of life. He promises no guarantees against cinders in the shoes, against falls, against blows from unsportsmanlike opponents. Eric Liddell promises deepest joy from the belief and practice of Christian love unending. He invites us all to become gentle knights, to experience the thrill of breaking the tape as God's joyful runner!